PowerShell for Beginners

Learn PowerShell 7 Through Hands-On Mini Games

Ian Waters

Apress®

PowerShell for Beginners: Learn PowerShell 7 Through Hands-On Mini Games

Ian Waters
Bexhill, UK

ISBN-13 (pbk): 978-1-4842-7063-9   ISBN-13 (electronic): 978-1-4842-7064-6
https://doi.org/10.1007/978-1-4842-7064-6

Managing Director, Apress Media LLC: Welmoed Spahr
Acquisitions Editor: Smriti Srivastava
Development Editor: Matthew Moodie
Coordinating Editor: Shrikant Vishwakarma

Cover designed by eStudioCalamar

Cover image designed by Pexels

Distributed to the book trade worldwide by Springer Science+Business Media LLC, 1 New York Plaza, Suite 4600, New York, NY 10004. Phone 1-800-SPRINGER, fax (201) 348-4505, e-mail orders-ny@springer-sbm.com, or visit www.springeronline.com. Apress Media, LLC is a California LLC and the sole member (owner) is Springer Science + Business Media Finance Inc (SSBM Finance Inc). SSBM Finance Inc is a **Delaware** corporation.

For information on translations, please e-mail booktranslations@springernature.com; for reprint, paperback, or audio rights, please e-mail bookpermissions@springernature.com, or visit http://www.apress.com/rights-permissions.

Apress titles may be purchased in bulk for academic, corporate, or promotional use. eBook versions and licenses are also available for most titles. For more information, reference our Print and eBook Bulk Sales web page at http://www.apress.com/bulk-sales.

Any source code or other supplementary material referenced by the author in this book is available to readers on GitHub via the book's product page, located at www.apress.com/978-1-4842-7063-9. For more detailed information, please visit http://www.apress.com/source-code.

Printed on acid-free paper

Many thanks to my wife for putting up with yet another project of mine. She gives me so much support. Thank you!

Also I dedicate this book to all those engineers and developers who want to develop their own skills, learn new technology, and share it with others.

Never stop learning!

Table of Contents

About the Author

 **Ian Waters** owns and runs Southern IT Networks Ltd with his business partner providing the best technical support for their clients across the United Kingdom. Ian has 16 years of experience in IT where he has developed a huge amount of expertise working with the following: Azure, Microsoft 365, PowerShell, Windows Server, Exchange, Cyber Security, and many more.

Ian loves retro gaming and software development, and these passions shine through in this book.

He is a frequent blogger and posts articles related to Microsoft's new technologies and projects to share his wealth of experience and knowledge with other engineers and developers.

Community contributions from him can be found at:

@Blog: www.slashadmin.co.uk/

@Facebook: www.facebook.com/SlashAdminLifeInIT

@Twitter: https://twitter.com/ijwaters

@Coderepo: https://github.com/slashadminsource

About the Technical Reviewer

Vikas Sukhija has over a decade of IT infrastructure experience with expertise in messaging, collaboration, and IT automation. He is a blogger, architect, and Microsoft MVP and is known as TechWizard. As an experienced professional, he assists small to large enterprises in architecting and implementing Office 365 and Azure.

Community contributions from him can be found at:

@Blog: `http://TechWizard.cloud`

@Page: `www.facebook.com/TechWizard.cloud`

@Twitter: `https://twitter.com/techwizardcloud`

@Coderepo: `https://github.com/VikasSukhija`

Introduction

Welcome to *PowerShell for Beginners*. I wanted to write this book to provide engineers and software developers a fun way to learn how to write scripts using PowerShell. My background is in IT support, I help to run an IT support company, and part of my job involves writing scripts to make our lives easier. Many of our own engineers struggle with scripting and struggle to learn the basics because it seems so daunting to get started and many find it boring. PowerShell really is easy to learn, and I've written this book to make it an enjoyable process by making it fun and engaging. Throughout this book, you are going to start with the very basics and learn what tools you need and how scripts can be structured and how you can write code to perform the tasks you need and build up your own useful set of PowerShell tools.

Each chapter will take you through a specific how-to guide, and each chapter will build on top of the previous chapters, and eventually you will start to write mini games old-school style!

If you are of a certain age over 30, then you will likely have fond memories of games with simple graphics but that were super fun. My favorite computers growing up were the BBC Micro, Amstrad CPC 464, and Amiga 500, and as a young boy, I enjoyed writing little games. No one ever played them, but I enjoyed doing it and learned to program much easier because it was fun and working out how to build something from nothing was rewarding.

Programming and writing scripts is a skill I still use to this day and will continue to use for the rest of my career in IT. The time you spend studying the content of this book will be well worth the time and effort.

I hope that this book works in the same way for you and provides you with a step-by-step guide on how to develop your own scripts and serves as a useful reference manual for the future. If you ever need to read or write to files in your script, just jump to Chapter 17 and dive in. If you need to add some sound, then jump to Chapter 18. This is a great book for learning the basics and for referring back to when you need them.

In previous books I've written, people have said, "Why do I need a book when I can learn everything I need from the Internet?" Well, you absolutely can and you should and will likely go looking for code on the Internet.

What's different with this book compared to articles on the Internet is that everything you need to get started is here. Everything is in one place and laid out in a specific way to accelerate your study of PowerShell and writing your own code.

All of the code has been checked and runs without errors, and all of the text has been verified by trusted experts in the field. Also, this book has been written with one aim all the way through, which is to learn PowerShell in a fun way without taking it or ourselves too seriously.

We will write code together, and you will begin to understand it, and you will start breaking it apart to build your own things. Steal any code in this book for your own projects, break it and modify it to automate tasks, or simply set up a networked version of PowerBomber in your office and see who will be the office champion! PowerBomber is one of the mini games you can build later in this book!

CHAPTER 1

Introduction

It's likely you don't need too much of an introduction to PowerShell because you purchased a book on how to write scripts and develop with it after all! First, we are going to dive into a little history, learn some terminology, and then get stuck into the fun part, writing code.

Essentially PowerShell is made up of a command line shell similar to that of the old DOS command prompt that can run code written in the PowerShell scripting language.

For years we Windows system administrators and script developers were using DOS-based batch scripts to automate tasks. Some of us started to dabble in VB scripts, which were more powerful but often difficult for many to master and understand and still lacked the power and flexibility that system administrators needed.

PowerShell is built on top of the .Net framework, which means you have access to a whole bunch of ready-made and high-level code, which means writing scripts is often easier in PowerShell than it once was trying to use a batch or VB script.

In this chapter, we will cover some basic PowerShell terminology that describes different PowerShell files and code structures and a little on how PowerShell came about and have a look at the future and lastly links to where you can download the two tools we will need to develop and run our PowerShell scripts.

Terminology

PowerShell has some unique terminology but for the most part follows the same conventions as many other programming languages. Code is written in a script file ending in .ps1 or module files ending in .psm1. Scripts and modules can contain variables, cmdlets, functions, and classes, which are different ways to work with and structure your code.

Let's take a brief look at each so you can start to get familiar with them because we will use these constantly throughout the book.

© Ian Waters 2021
I. Waters, *PowerShell for Beginners*, https://doi.org/10.1007/978-1-4842-7064-6_1

Variables

Variables are used to store values such as numbers, some text, a list, or a collection of other objects. When working with variables, we will generally define what type of information we are storing, followed by a name we will use to reference it, and often we will want to set a default value. Variables hold data, and we can use their names to write new data into them or to read the data out. We will cover variables in depth in Chapter 3.

Cmdlets

Cmdlets are commands that are built into PowerShell to perform specific functions. Cmdlets are typically grouped together into groups servicing different technologies. For example, there are groups of cmdlets built for working with Active Directory (AD), Azure AD, Office 365, and many more, and they are packed up into modules. If you need specific functionality, more than likely there is a module out there you can install and use in your projects. We are at the point now where many Microsoft products are first developed in PowerShell to provide functionality that graphical user interfaces are then built on top of, which is another benefit of learning PowerShell because some things can't be done in the UI of certain Microsoft products.

Cmdlets are typically typed directly into the PowerShell prompt to complete a specific function such as adding a new user into Microsoft 365, returning a list of users from Active Directory, or listing the contents of a folder on the system hard drive. You can write a script to group together many cmdlets to perform more advanced tasks.

Scripts

PowerShell scripts are files that can contain many cmdlets, functions, and classes and are used to write your own automated tasks or, in our case, fun little games. You will learn to write your own scripts, which may automate many tasks within your business, or maybe you really do want to write old-school games for the fun of it... Hey, I do!

Functions

These are sections of code that perform subtasks within your scripts. A subtask could be code that writes information out to a file. You can group all the code required to do this within a function and in your main code just call the function to perform the subtask. This is a great way to keep your code clean and easy to read. Divide your code up into functions.

Classes

Classes are a way to group code together to define an object. You may need to develop a script that scans a network and collects information about computers on the network. Using a class, you can define what information you need to know about each computer and save that information to use later. In the computer class, you can store the name, operating system version, how much disk space it has, and how much memory it has along with any other information you need to store about each computer. Then you create an instance of the class to create an object stored as a variable, and you can pass that object around your script to perform different tasks. Don't worry too much if this sounds confusing because we have a full chapter on it later in the book.

Modules

Modules are collections of PowerShell cmdlets, functions, variables, and classes all wrapped into a nice package called a module file ending in .psm1. There are many modules available to download and install, and each one adds extra functionality to your scripts. There are modules for working with the Microsoft Azure platform, modules for working with Amazon's AWS platform, and modules for working with databases, servers, and many more. If you are working with a specific product or platform, then chances are there are PowerShell modules to help you start developing scripts for it quicker and easier.

Objects

Everything in PowerShell is an object of some type or another. When you hear a reference to an object or a group of objects, it could be referring to a number variable, a collection of characters in a line of text, or a line of text itself, which is known as a string object.

An object can hold lots of information about what makes it, a string object will contain a list of character objects, and so on. In the real world, a car is an object; and cars are built up from lots of other objects, wheels, mirrors, lights, and so on. Each of these objects can have different properties that describe each of those parts such as color, weight, and material used to make it. The same is true when talking about objects in PowerShell. You can create variables that are objects of the specified type, and you can even use a class to create a complicated object containing lots of other objects.

Pipeline

In code, you may see the | symbol, which refers to the pipeline operator. The pipeline operator is used to pass the results of the code from the left side to the code on the right. You can use the pipeline operator to pass the results from multiple commands to the next in a long line. Some cmdlets require you to pipe information to them using the pipeline operator.

.Net Framework

The .Net framework is a free developer platform that gives us a vast range of prebuilt objects and code to use in our own scripts. In fact, PowerShell is built on top of the .Net framework, which means we can leverage the .Net framework to implement features and functionality that may otherwise require us to write thousands of lines of code to implement ourselves.

History

Way back in 2001, Microsoft started working on something to replace the aging DOS command prompt and to have a new way to develop scripts. They started working on a new shell, which was called Monad, and in 2002 a white paper called the Monad Manifesto was published that outlined the goals for the project and the issues it set out to solve. In the manifesto, they state that Monad is the next-generation platform for administrative automation that utilizes the .Net platform.

To run scripts, they developed the Monad shell, which is a .Net-based script execution environment for running scripts and cmdlets. This shell is what we now commonly refer to as the PowerShell prompt or PowerShell console.

Then in 2006 Microsoft formally renamed the Monad project to PowerShell and released version 1 of the PowerShell programming language.

PowerShell has become so embraced by the community and Microsoft that it's become built into the Windows operating system ever since, and the latest version shipped with Windows is PowerShell 5.1.

PowerShell was continually developed and new versions released until Microsoft announced on August 18, 2016, a new version called PowerShell Core. At this time, Microsoft announced that the project would be made open source and cross-platform. This means that you can develop scripts for Windows, Mac, and several flavors of Linux including Ubuntu, which is awesome.

In this book, we are going to be focusing on PowerShell 7 because it's the first release that really focuses on the future direction of PowerShell to be open source, multiplatform, and even more backward compatible to older versions. It's good to note that if you run a Windows computer, PowerShell will likely come preinstalled, with the older Windows having only version 5.1. PowerShell 7 is a different beast and as such needs installing separately.

The Future

There is no doubt that PowerShell has matured enough and now becomes so accessible with it being baked into the Windows operating system and runs across many different platforms that it's the preferred method of scripting in the enterprise environment. You are going to do very well by learning how to proficiently develop your own scripts, and it's going to be a skill that will look great on your CV. Even small IT firms/teams regularly have a need to write PowerShell scripts for their clients or own businesses, needing to automate SQL backups, copy files around the network, and remotely run code on devices on the network. There is a whole world of problems and manual tasks you will be able to automate using the knowledge you will gain in this book.

Required Tools

You will need to download and install the latest version of PowerShell, which is version 7 at the time of writing:

```
https://github.com/PowerShell/PowerShell/releases
```

Since we are working with the cutting-edge technologies, we need a fully featured development environment to write our scripts in and run them. For this we will use Visual Studio Code, Microsoft's cross-platform development tool available for Windows, Mac OS, and Linux:

```
https://code.visualstudio.com/
```

Let's Get Started!

Ok, that's the intro to the book and a short history of PowerShell finished. You are going to learn to write scripts using PowerShell 7 and the Visual Studio Code development tool, and hopefully you will find it easy, engaging, and fun.

Settle in and let's get started!

## CHAPTER 2

Beginners' Guide to PowerShell and Visual Studio Code

Getting started developing PowerShell scripts is very easy, and the tools you need are open source and free to download and use. We first need to install the latest version of PowerShell and the code development tool Visual Studio Code.

PowerShell 7

PowerShell is the scripting language but also a command line shell that runs the scripting language. So we first need to install PowerShell in order to run our scripts. Remember PowerShell is open source and multiplatform making it extremely versatile but is not yet installed by default on many systems, so it's an additional component that needs to be downloaded and installed to make use of it. Windows 10 comes with the older version PowerShell 5.1, but this is no longer maintained. Although many of the scripts and teachings in this book will work with the Windows built-in version, there are several PowerShell 7 coding features that are not present in older versions, so ensure you get the latest version and install it.

Install PowerShell 7

Browse to `https://github.com/PowerShell/powershell/releases` and scroll down until you find the install files. As shown in Figure 2-1, you will find installers for lots of different operating systems, so download the one for your platform.

© Ian Waters 2021
I. Waters, *PowerShell for Beginners*, https://doi.org/10.1007/978-1-4842-7064-6_2

Figure 2-1. *PowerShell repository on GitHub*

In this book, I'll be using Windows 10, so I download the PowerShell-7.1.0-win-x64.msi file and begin the install process shown in Figure 2-2.

Figure 2-2. *Installing PowerShell 7 on Windows*

Click Next through the installation until you get to the Optional Actions screen shown in Figure 2-3.

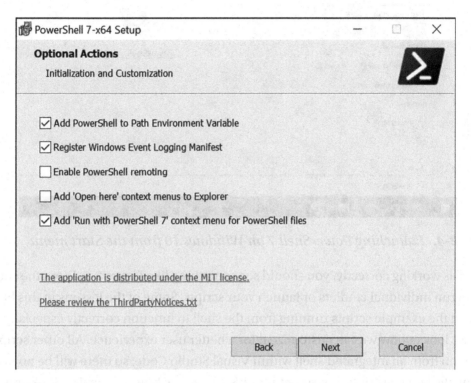

Figure 2-3. *Installing PowerShell 7 on Windows – Optional Actions*

Here, I like to select the option "Add 'Run with PowerShell 7' context menu for PowerShell files." This option lets you run PowerShell script files directly using PowerShell 7, saving you from having to load up PowerShell and then locate and run the script.

Now it's time to fire up the shell!

Be sure to run PowerShell version 7.1 from your system. If you are using Windows 10, it will come with PowerShell version 5.1, so be sure to run the correct version to ensure you can run all of the scripts and code examples presented in this book without error. On my Windows 10 system, I open the Start menu and type PowerShell 7, and it shows at the top of the program list as shown in Figure 2-4.

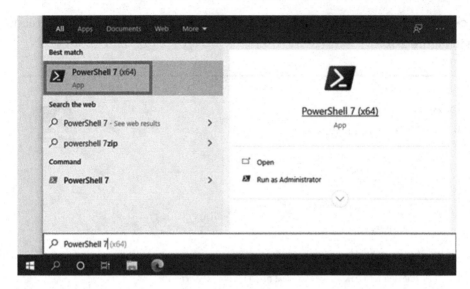

Figure 2-4. *Launching PowerShell 7 on Windows 10 from the Start menu*

If all is working correctly, you should see something like Figure 2-5. From the shell, you can run individual cmdlets or launch your scripts. Some of the lessons in this book will need the example scripts running from the shell to function correctly especially when we look at how we can customize it for a better user experience. All other scripts will be run from an integrated shell within Visual Studio Code, so there will be no need to manually launch scripts, but sometimes it's nice to see how your scripts look and behave when run from the shell.

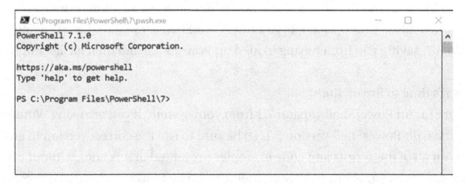

Figure 2-5. *PowerShell 7 console*

Let's start by running a simple cmdlet to find out which version of PowerShell you have installed. To do this, type Get-Host and press Enter. This cmdlet returns the version number and other useful information about how PowerShell is configured on your system.

On my system, I have version 7.1.0, good because that's what we just installed and this cmdlet confirms it as shown in Figure 2-6.

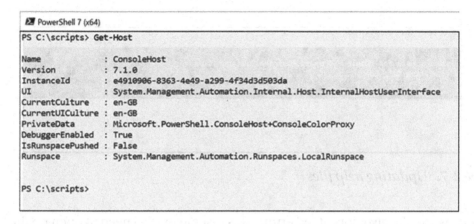

Figure 2-6. *PowerShell 7 console running the Get-Host cmdlet*

Congratulations! You just ran your first cmdlet!

Get Help Running Cmdlets

Sometimes you will see a cmdlet that looks interesting, or maybe you are having trouble running a cmdlet successfully. Well, there is a cmdlet for that: Get-Help followed by the cmdlet you want help with. Or you can use the shortcut and just type Help and then the cmdlet name. Some built-in cmdlets have alternative names called an alias; Help is an alias of Get-Help. The alias is usually shorter and easier to remember but ultimately calls the same cmdlet.

Before you try that, first, update the help files on your PC by running the cmdlet Update-Help. This will ensure you have all of the latest help files on your system. If you run this cmdlet and experience issues where help files are not updating, it may be because help files are not available in your language or region yet. Specifying the parameter UICulture with en-US tells the cmdlet to download the English US–specific help files, which are generally more available. On my system, I needed to run the cmdlet like this to get everything updated:

```
Update-Help -UICulture en-US
```

Figure 2-7 shows the cmdlet running and updating the help files.

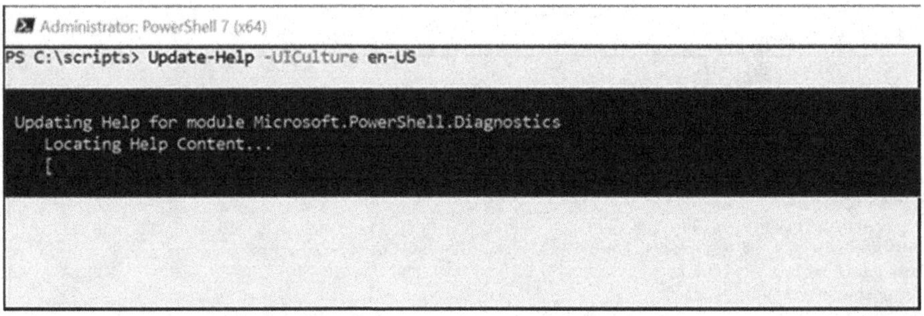

Figure 2-7. *Updating help files*

Don't worry if it gives lots of red errors; this just means you need to open up the PowerShell console by running it as an administrator. Close the window, then right-click the PowerShell icon in the Start menu, and select "Run as Administrator" and confirm any prompts that come up. Now run the cmdlet Update-Help again. It's common to still get a few errors as these are usually due to it not being able to locate update files for particular PowerShell modules. Modules are simply a package of cmdlets, which are used to administrate a particular system, for example, Azure AD. We will talk about these in the next section.

Ok, so you find a cmdlet that looks interesting for a project you are working on, but you want to find out more about it. Cmdlets can be passed information to change what they do. To get a detailed description of a cmdlet, simply run Get-Help followed by the cmdlet. I've found an interesting cmdlet called Get-Process, and I want to know more about it, so I run Get-Help Get-Process.

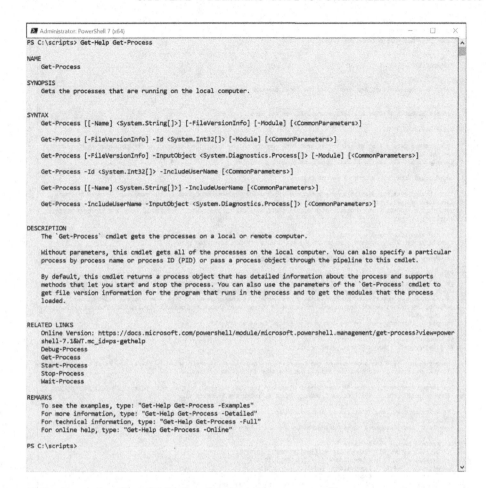

Figure 2-8. *Running Get-Help for the Get-Process cmdlet*

As you can see in Figure 2-8, it returns lots of information on what parameters can be set and includes a description and related cmdlets and even shows you how to get example commands in the REMARKS section by running Get-Help Get-Process -examples.

Cmdlets can have parameters, which are built-in settings. Here, adding -examples to the end of the cmdlet tells Get-Help to output examples of how to run it. More on how cmdlets work in the next chapter.

Let's run and see what we get with Get-Help Get-Process -examples.

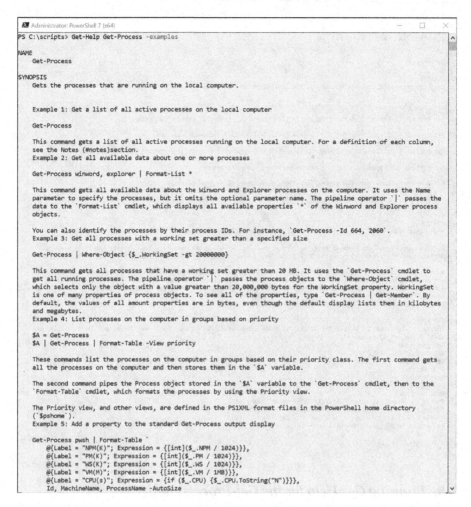

Figure 2-9. *Examples for the Get-Process cmdlet*

As you can see in Figure 2-9, it provides a whole bunch of useful examples you can use in your own projects. If you struggle to find examples online, then remember these useful cmdlets because they contain great nuggets of information you won't easily find online.

How to Run Scripts

PowerShell scripts are plaintext files that contain lines of code and are often built up of multiple cmdlets, functions, and classes – things you will learn about in this book later. For now, here is a very simple script you can create yourself and run.

Open up Notepad, Word, or your favorite text editor and write the following three cmdlets in the file. The Write-Host cmdlet outputs text, which is passed out to the PowerShell console window.

Save the file into a scripts folder on your C drive as c:\scripts\Hello.ps1 as shown in Figure 2-10.

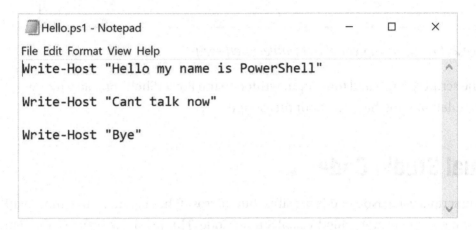

Figure 2-10. *Example PowerShell script written in Notepad*

There are three ways to run a script file. The script won't run just by typing the name of the file. You must use one of the following methods. The first is by typing the full path to the file, c:\scripts\Hello.ps1, and pressing Enter.

The second way is to navigate to the folder that stores your scripts and run them just by typing .\<scriptname.ps1>. In our example here, just type .\hello.ps1 and press Enter.

It's a pain having to type the full path to the file every time you want to run a script. Instead, the third way is you can navigate to a different folder in the same way you can using a command prompt.

Simply type cd c:\scripts and press Enter.

Your working directory will change to c:\scripts, and you can now run any script in that folder as shown in Figure 2-11.

```
Administrator: PowerShell 7 (x64)
PS C:\scripts> .\Hello.ps1
Hello my name is PowerShell
Cant talk now
Bye
PS C:\scripts>
```

Figure 2-11. *Running your first PowerShell script*

The script will run and the output written to the PowerShell console window. Congratulations! You have run your first script!

Visual Studio Code

Writing scripts using Notepad is possible, but Microsoft has created a free multiplatform development application called Visual Studio Code. This means we can use the same tool when using Windows, Mac, or Linux. You will use this tool to write most of the scripts in this book. It makes script development so much easier, and some of the reasons include the following:

- One program to write scripts and run them.

- Code is formatted with different colors making it easy to read.

- Full scripts or highlighted sections of code can be run right from the application.

- Includes built-in help files.

- Highlights syntax errors (code not written correctly).

Install Visual Studio Code

To install Visual Studio Code, browse to `https://code.visualstudio.com` and download the latest version for your operating system. Figure 2-12 shows the site has detected I'm on a Windows system and offers the latest version for my system.

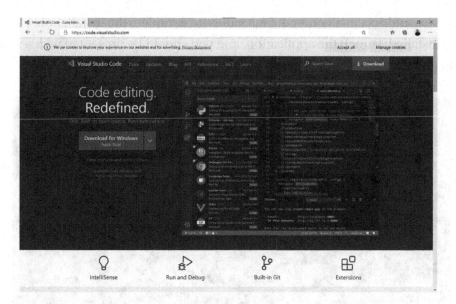

Figure 2-12. *Downloading Visual Studio Code*

Install the program and accept all defaults until you get to the Select Additional Tasks page shown in Figure 2-13. On here, select all of the options so you can open PowerShell files directly in Visual Studio Code.

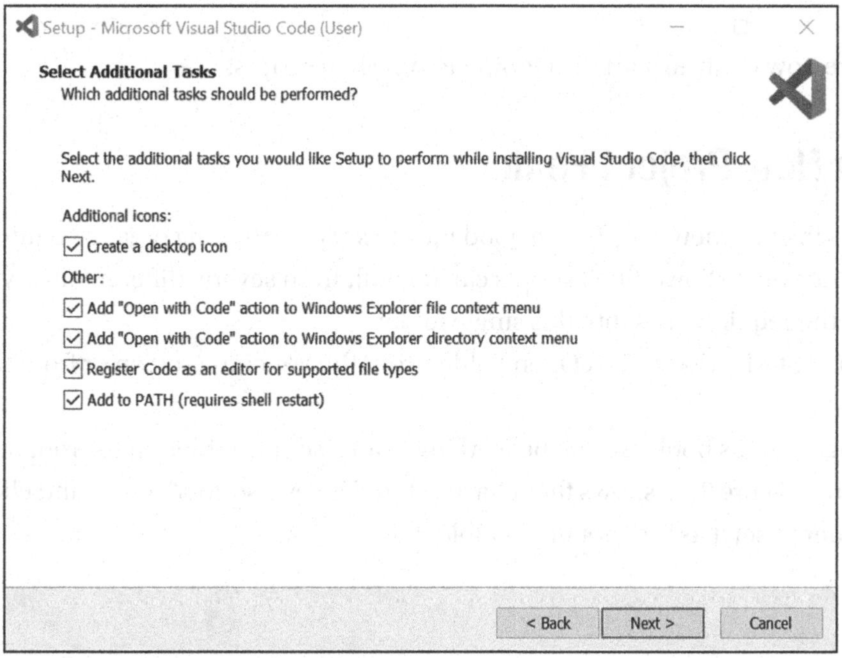

Figure 2-13. *Installing Visual Studio Code*

17

Click Next and accept all other default values to complete the installation.

Once installed, launch the application, and you should be presented with a window similar to that shown in Figure 2-14.

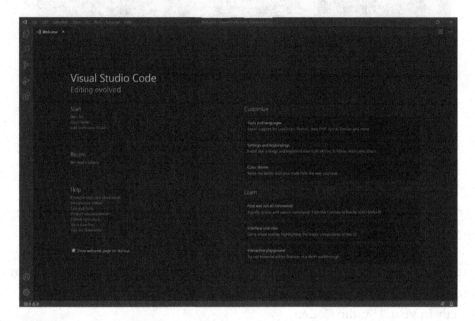

Figure 2-14. *Launching Visual Studio Code*

You are now ready to start developing PowerShell scripts!

Open a New Project Folder

When working on a new script, it's a good idea to keep everything organized into a single project folder. Since PowerShell scripts can be built from several different files, you can save all of the required files into this single folder.

In Visual Studio Code, click Open Folder from the Welcome screen or from the File menu.

Throughout this book, we will be working from a scripts folder on the root of the system drive. Figure 2-15 shows that I have created a new "scripts" folder and clicked Select Folder to set it as the root project folder.

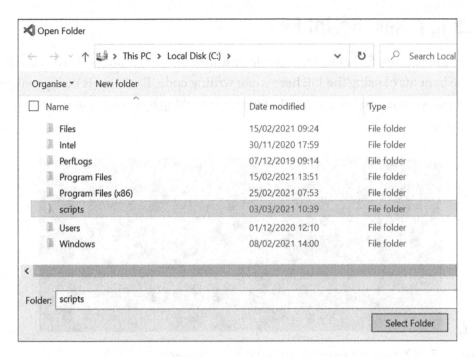

Figure 2-15. *Opening a project folder*

In the top-left corner shown in Figure 2-16, you will now see the scripts folder. In here you can create new folders and new script files needed for your projects. Next, we will look at what each of the buttons to the right of the folder does.

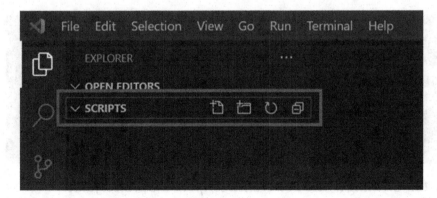

Figure 2-16. *Viewing contents of the scripts project folder and available actions*

Creating a New Script File

To create a new script file, click the new file button shown in Figure 2-17. You can start to see the benefits of using the ISE here when writing code. Each line is numbered, and different parts of the code show in different colors making it easy to read scripts and debug errors.

Figure 2-17. *Creating a new file in the project folder*

You will be prompted to give the new file a name and extension. Since we are working with PowerShell scripts, the extension is .ps1. After you name the file, it will open in the editor ready for you to start developing your scripts as shown in Figure 2-18.

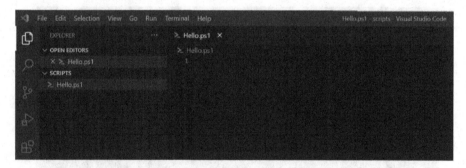

Figure 2-18. *Creating a new PowerShell script in the project folder*

PowerShell Visual Studio Code Extension

When you first open up a PowerShell file, Visual Studio Code will ask if you wish to install the extensions. Extensions bring new features and functionality, which is why Visual Studio Code has become so popular. It's multiplatform but also able to work with a wide variety of languages and other tools via the use of extensions.

When prompted, click Install to add the extensions as shown in Figure 2-19.

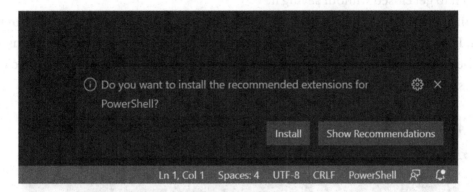

Figure 2-19. *Installing the PowerShell extensions*

Clicking Install will take you to the Extensions menu, which will list all currently installed extensions. If you have a fresh install of Visual Studio Code, you should now see the PowerShell extension installed shown in Figure 2-20.

Figure 2-20. *Viewing installed extensions*

Now that Visual Studio Code has the extension installed, it will understand the PowerShell language, how to run it, and how to highlight the code in different colors correctly, and also it will enable IntelliSense, which is a great feature that pops up

21

suggested code based on what you are typing. So if you start typing a cmdlet, it will show you different parameters you can set. This makes writing scripts so much easier and saves you hunting for help on how to run cmdlets.

Saving Scripts

Remember to regularly save your scripts. Nothing worse than spending hours on code only for it to get closed without saving it.

In the new Hello.ps1 script, I call the Write-Host cmdlet followed by text in quotation marks. This cmdlet will write the text in quotation marks out to the PowerShell console. Next, we will see how to run this script, but for now, click File and then Save to save the changes as shown in Figure 2-21.

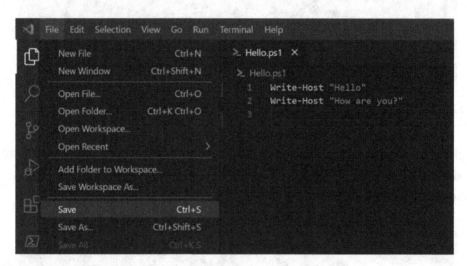

Figure 2-21. Saving a script

Running Scripts

Visual Studio Code integrates the PowerShell shell into the program making it easier to test snippets of code and run full scripts. Before we do anything else, locate the terminal window at the bottom of Visual Studio Code and type in $PSVersionTable and press Enter. If everything is working correctly, it should return the version of PowerShell you installed as shown in Figure 2-22. In this case, it's reporting back 7.1.0 correctly, which is the version installed earlier in this chapter.

```
PROBLEMS    OUTPUT    DEBUG CONSOLE    TERMINAL
PS C:\scripts> $PSVersionTable


Name                          Value
----                          -----
PSVersion                     7.1.0
PSEdition                     Core
GitCommitId                   7.1.0
OS                            Microsoft Windows 10.0.19042
Platform                      Win32NT
PSCompatibleVersions          {1.0, 2.0, 3.0, 4.0…}
PSRemotingProtocolVersion     2.3
SerializationVersion          1.1.0.1
WSManStackVersion             3.0

PS C:\scripts> █
```

Figure 2-22. *Confirming the PowerShell version*

Running Your First Script

To run the currently selected script, click Run and then Run Without Debugging shown in Figure 2-23. This will run the script in the terminal window at the bottom of Visual Studio Code just as if you were running it from within a normal PowerShell shell.

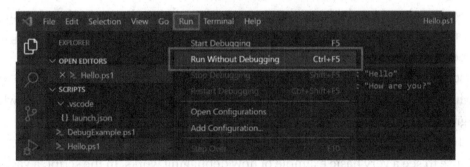

Figure 2-23. *Run a script without debugging*

You can see the output of the script in the terminal window in Figure 2-24, and the Write-Host cmdlets output the text directly to the console window.

```
PROBLEMS    OUTPUT    DEBUG CONSOLE    TERMINAL

=====> PowerShell Integrated Console v2020.6.0 <=====

PS C:\scripts> c:\scripts\Hello.ps1
Hello
How are you?
PS C:\scripts> █
```

Figure 2-24. *Running your first script in Visual Studio Code*

Congratulations! You've just run your first script within Visual Studio Code!

Debugging Your Scripts

Now we need to configure Visual Studio Code debugging. Debugging scripts is vital when trying to work out why things don't behave as you expect them to. Believe me this happens a lot even to experienced coders, but especially for beginners when learning how things work. By using the debugging tools, you can stop your code at specific points and view the values of variables or the outcome of conditions in your scripts. Looking at the values of variables then helps you work out why things are not quite running as expected, which is very useful.

First, we need to configure a Run and Debug configuration file "launch.json." This is a file where Visual Studio Code stores information about settings you want to use when debugging your scripts.

In the following example, I create a new PowerShell script DebugExample.ps1, which we will use to see a very basic example of how debugging works. In the script, a variable $number is assigned the value 1; then it's written out to the screen using the Write-Host cmdlet. Then the $number variable is assigned the next number in the sequence and displayed on the screen again, and this repeats a few times.

Click the debug and run icon from the left-hand menu and then click "create a launch.json file" as shown in Figure 2-25.

Figure 2-25. *Configuring a debug configuration file*

Now select "Launch Current File" from the debug configuration selection drop-down list as shown in Figure 2-26. This option tells Visual Studio Code that when you select Run and Debug, you want to run the file you are currently working on.

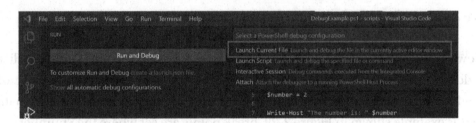

Figure 2-26. *Configuring Run and Debug to launch the current file*

This will open up the launch.json file shown in Figure 2-27 with the configuration to run debugging with the currently selected PowerShell file. You can close the file and saving changes is prompted. We won't need to edit this file any further, but it will appear in the Explorer window so it can be changed in the future if needed.

```
                    • launch.json - scripts - Visual Studio Code
 ≥ DebugExample.ps1         {} launch.json  •

.vscode > {} launch.json > ...
    1   {
    2       // Use IntelliSense to learn about possible attributes.
    3       // Hover to view descriptions of existing attributes.
    4       // For more information, visit: https://go.microsoft.com/fwlink/?linkid=830387
    5       "version": "0.2.0",
    6       "configurations": [
    7           {
    8               "name": "PowerShell: Launch Current File",
    9               "type": "PowerShell",
   10               "request": "launch",
   11               "script": "${file}",
   12               "cwd": "${file}"
   13           }
   14       ]
   15   }
   16   |
```

Figure 2-27. *Debug configuration launch.json file*

Now click the blank areas to the left of the line numbers in the script and left-click. This adds a red circle to the start of the line, and this is called a break point. Break points are used to stop the execution of code at a specific line before running the code on it.

In this example shown in Figure 2-28, break points are set where the $number variable gets assigned new values. This will make the script stop at these points, and Visual Studio Code will show us the value of all variables in our script up to that point.

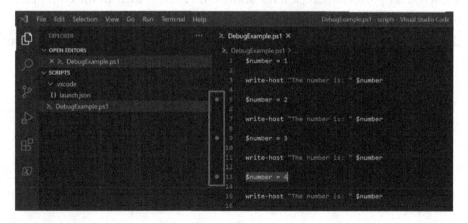

Figure 2-28. *Setting break points*

```
$number = 1

Write-Host "The number is: " $number

$number = 2

Write-Host "The number is: " $number

$number = 3

Write-Host "The number is: " $number

$number = 4

Write-Host "The number is: " $number
```

Ok, with the break points set on the $number variable, click Run from the main menu bar and click "Start Debugging" or press F5 as shown in Figure 2-29.

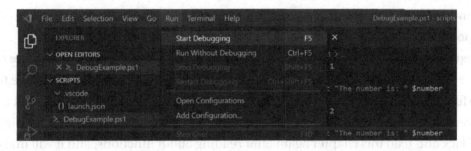

Figure 2-29. *Debugging a script*

Now the script will run, and it will pause at the first break point set in the code as shown in Figure 2-30.

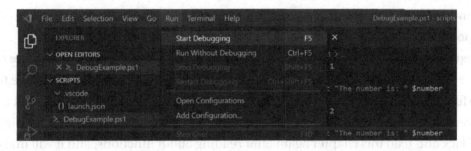

Figure 2-30. *Viewing the value of variables*

Now for the really useful bit, look in the Variables window and find the $number variable. You can see it's showing a value of 1, which is exactly what we are expecting. The break point stopped the code before the $number variable was updated to 2. This is extremely useful when trying to figure out whether variables contain the information you expect them to and use that to fix your code.

When a break point is reached you can control how the code continues using the debugging toolbar shown in Figure 2-31.

Figure 2-31. *The debugging control panel*

The icons in the toolbar work as follows.

Continue (F5): Executes the rest of the script normally and exist unless it hits another breakpoint.

Step Over (F10) – Executes the next line of code and pauses until you continue or step over the next line of code again. If your code reaches a function, it will execute the whole function and then pause on the next line. (Don't worry about knowing what a function is just yet. You will understand what they are soon, but remember this point and come back and read this chapter again after reading about functions, and it will make more sense and be more useful then.)

Step Into (F11) – Similar to Step Over where it will execute the next line of code and pause. Only this time if the code enters a function, it will go into that function and pause at the next line in it rather than execute everything in the function and pause at the line after it.

Step Out (Shift + F11) – If you use the Step Into button to go to the code inside a function, you can use Step Out to execute all of the remaining code within it and stop at the next line from where the function was called from. This is useful if you want to see what the code within a function looks like and does, and then you can jump out of it easily using this command.

Restart (Ctrl + Shift + F5) – This will stop the script and run it again from the start. Useful when trying to debug specific sections of code. You can keep repeating the debug procedure and look at the values of different variables each time more easily.

Stop (Shift + F5) – Stops the script immediately and stops debugging.

Debugging is extremely useful when writing code and trying to figure out why parts of it don't work correctly. This feature is another reason why Visual Studio Code is so popular with coders at all skill levels.

Running Part of a Script

Sometimes you want to test part of a script rather than running the whole thing. This can be very useful when working on long scripts and can make debugging easier.

Simply highlight a single line or multiple lines of code, right-click, and select "Run Selection" or press F8 as shown in Figure 2-32.

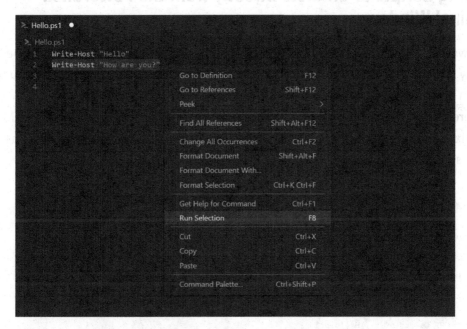

Figure 2-32. *Running only selected code*

This will run the selected line or lines of code in the terminal window shown in Figure 2-33.

This is great when trying to write code to perform a specific task and saves you having to run the whole script and using break points. Simply select the new code and run the selection.

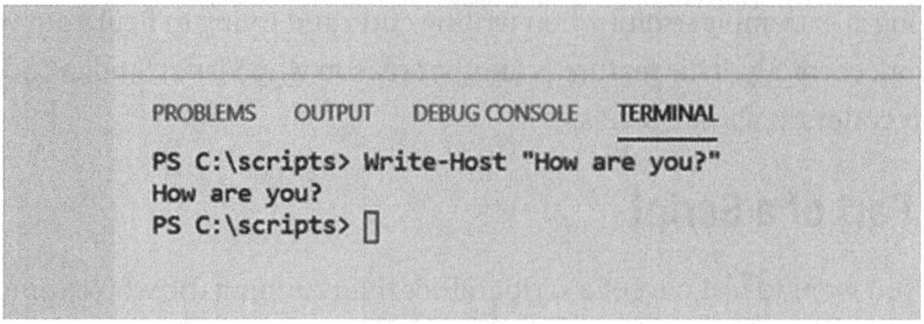

```
PROBLEMS    OUTPUT    DEBUG CONSOLE    TERMINAL

PS C:\scripts> Write-Host "How are you?"
How are you?
PS C:\scripts> []
```

Figure 2-33. *Running cmdlets directly in the terminal window*

Running Scripts or Cmdlets Directly from the PowerShell Terminal Window

If you want to quickly test the output of a single line of code or cmdlet, you can type it directly into the PowerShell terminal window and press Enter. The line of code you type will run just as it would in a standalone PowerShell console window.

Here I type dir to display the contents of the c:\scripts folder. Type ls if using a Mac or Linux. Then I run the script Hello.ps1 by typing .\Hello.ps1 and pressing Enter as demonstrated in Figure 2-34.

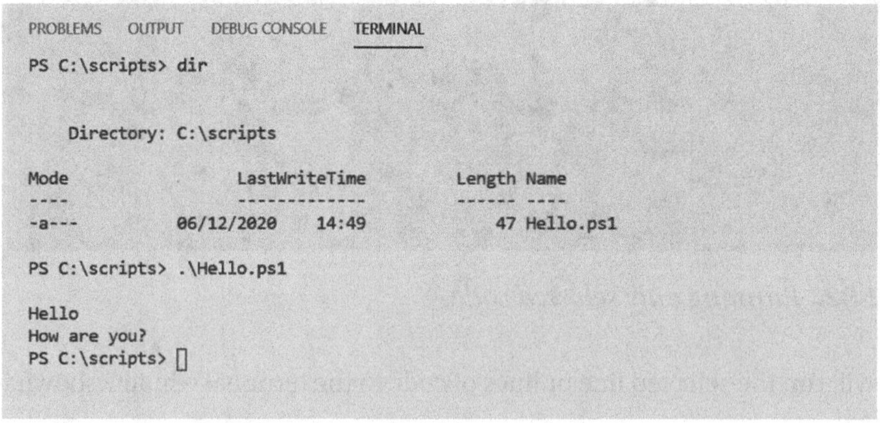

```
PROBLEMS    OUTPUT    DEBUG CONSOLE    TERMINAL

PS C:\scripts> dir


    Directory: C:\scripts

Mode                 LastWriteTime         Length Name
----                 -------------         ------ ----
-a---          06/12/2020     14:49            47 Hello.ps1

PS C:\scripts> .\Hello.ps1

Hello
How are you?
PS C:\scripts> []
```

Figure 2-34. *Running scripts from the terminal window*

Have a play yourself and run the following cmdlets to see the output.

Get-Command lists all of the cmdlets available to you in the current session. You can add more commands by loading modules as we will see later.

Write-Host "Hello" displays Hello to the screen.

Get-Host displays the version of PowerShell being used.

Clear-Host clears everything off the console window.

Adding Comments to Your Code

Adding comments to your code is very important as it will help you understand your code better when you come back to it after a few months. Also when someone else reads your code, they will follow what the code does easier. I quite often start a new piece of code by breaking it up into sections and writing out comments. In the code, I'll start with a standard comment block called "comment-based help," which tells people what the script does and gives examples of how to run it. Next, I'll add comments that say something like #Program variables, and here I will list off the variables I'm going to use. In another section, I might write #Get data from database, and the code following it will do exactly that. These are only small examples, but when writing your own code, add lots of comments and even use comment blocks when you need to explain what a section of code does in detail.

Comment sections in your code are not executed, so you can use those areas to write any notes you need to help people know what the code does and how each section works.

Comment-Based Help

Comment-based help sections are used at the top of scripts to tell people what the script does, give examples of how to run the script, and tell people what objects they can pass into the script and what objects get returned as output.

```
<#
  .SYNOPSIS
  Says hello to anyone who runs this script.

  .DESCRIPTION
  The Hello.ps1 script prints our Hello how are you to the screen.

  .PARAMETER Name
  Specifies the name of the person running the script.
```

```
.INPUTS
 None. You cannot pipe objects to Hello.ps1.

.OUTPUTS
 Writes two string objects "Hello" and "How are you?" to the console.

.EXAMPLE
 C:\PS> .\Hello.ps1

.EXAMPLE
 C:\PS> .\Hello.ps1 -Name Ian
#>
```

Single-Line Comments

To add a single-line comment, start it with a # symbol, and everything on that line will become a comment and turn green. Single-line comments are great for adding small notes about a section of code or to highlight what a small section of code does.

```
# This is a single line comment
```

Multiline Comments

To create a large section of comments called a "code block," start with <# and end it with #>. A code block can span several lines, and they are great for adding very detailed comments to your code. They are especially useful if you end up writing something that is quite complicated.

```
<#
    This is a comment block.
    You can use a comment block to write notes across multiple lines
#>
```

Conclusion

You now have the basic skills required to develop, debug, and run your PowerShell scripts using PowerShell 7 and Visual Studio Code. You have everything you need to start writing awesome scripts, so let's now move on and start learning the PowerShell scripting language.

CHAPTER 3

Variables

In this chapter, we are going to learn one of the most important parts of any script or program, variables! We are going to learn how they are used to store information and how they can be accessed and manipulated from different sections of your code. Variables come in many different types, and each type has specific ways to store and access the data.

I've bundled the code listed in this chapter into one file rather than having lots of small files to make it easy for you to try each of the examples by highlighting the code and choosing "Run Selection" within Visual Studio Code.

```
# Common Variable Types
[string]$name       = "Peter"
# strings are a 'string of' characters making a word or sentance.
[char]$letter       = 'A'
# char type are single characters.
[bool]$isEnabled    = $false
# bool type can be $true or $false.
[int]$age           = 37
# int type is a whole number.
[decimal]$height    = 12345.23
# decimal type allows large numbers with decimals.
[double]$var        = 54321.21
# similar to decimal but is a 8 byte decimal floating point number.
[single]$var        = 76549.11
# similar to decimal but is a 32 bit floating point number.
[long]$var          = 2382.22
# similar to decimal bus is a 64 bit integer.
```

© Ian Waters 2021
I. Waters, *PowerShell for Beginners*, https://doi.org/10.1007/978-1-4842-7064-6_3

```
[DateTime]$birthday = "Feburary 12, 1982"
# Date and time value.
[array]$var        = "itemone", "itemtwo"
# Indexed list of objects, in this case an array of string values but they
  can be any other object type.
[hashtable]$var    = @{Name = "Ian"; Age = 37; Height = 5.9 }
# Name and Value pairs. You can mix variable types.

# If you dont specify the variable type PowerShell will determine the best
  fit.
$myVariable = "hello this is a string variable"

# It's best practice to always specify the variable type
[string]$myVariable = "hello this is a string variable"

# Assigning the number 5 to the int variable $numberVariable
[int]$numberVariable = 5

# Assigning $true value to the $booleanVariable
[bool]$booleanVariable = $true

# If you create a variable of a specific type then try assigning an
  incompatiable value it will result in an error.
[int]$age = 3
$age = "old"

# You can overwrite existing values by assigning a new one at any time.
$age = 38
$age = 83
$age = 23

# You can display the value of a variable to the console buy simply typeing
  the variable name.
[int]$age = 37
$age

# If you want to write text to the console in a flexiable way use the
  Write-Host cmdlet.
Write-Host "It's my birthday and i'm " $age
```

```
#Global variables can be used to allow access to them across your script
#Player position
[int]$global:xPosition = 4
[int]$global:yPosition = 3
$global:xPosition
```

Let's dive in.

What Are Variables?

Variables are used to store values into memory and within your scripts. Variables can hold numbers, sentences that we call strings, and any other type of object that is used to store information. Variables can be used to collect values from user input to be used in the script or can be used to capture the output from a cmdlet. Variables are typically defined at the top of your scripts and often given initial values. Then within the script, the values stored in these variables can be read, updated, or passed into another part of the script to have another action performed with the information.

Variable Types

There are several predefined variable types you can use, and some you will use all of the time and others less so.

If you want to store a sentence or string of characters, you define a [string] variable. Variable types are put into square brackets at the start of the variable followed by the name you give the variable and then a default value to set to it.

Variable type	Example	Notes
[string]	[string]$name = "Peter"	A string of characters
[char]	[char]$letter = 'A'	Individual characters
[bool]	[bool]$isEnabled = $false	True or false values
[int]	[int]$age = 37	32-bit integer/general whole numbers

Variable type	Example	Notes
[decimal]	[decimal]$height = 12345.23	128-bit values Minimum value: -79228162514264337593543950335 Maximum value: 79228162514264337593543950335
[double]	[double]$var = 54321.21	8-byte decimal floating-point numbers
[single]	[single]$var = 76549.11	32-bit floating-point numbers
[long]	[long]$var = 2382.22	64-bit integers
[DateTime]	[DateTime]$birthday = "February 12, 1982"	Date and time values
[array]	[array]$var = "itemone", "itemtwo"	Indexed list of values. You can mix variable types
[hashtable]	[hashtable]$var = @{Name = "Ian"; Age = 37; Height = 5.9 }	Name and value pairs. You can mix variable types

Defining Variables

To set up a variable in your script, simply use the $ symbol followed by the name you wish to use and then assign a value to it.

Let's create a variable to hold a string of characters (a sentence):

```
$myVariable = "hello this is a string variable"
```

Variables always start with a $ symbol followed by their name. Values are assigned to variables using the = symbol.

In PowerShell, the variable type will be set automatically based on the value you assign to it. In the preceding example, $myVariable will be set up with the type [string] because we have set its value to a string "hello this is a string variable".

This is nice behavior, but it's not easy to work out what type the variable is when reading scripts. I always prefer to set the type of a variable manually as follows:

```
[string]$myVariable = "hello this is a string variable"
```

If you want to set up a variable to hold a number, use

```
[int]$numberVariable = 5
```

This is another useful example. Let's say you want a variable to hold a yes or no or true or false value. For this, we use the [bool] variable type:

```
[bool]$booleanVariable = $true
```

In PowerShell, true and false values are built into the language and always are used like this: $true and $false.

If you want to retrieve the value of a variable, you can use the variable name within the script anywhere you need it.

You can reference the preceding table to quickly see how to define the different variable types. You will learn how to define different variable types as we move through the chapters in this book.

Updating Variables

You can update variables by assigning a new value to them just as you can when you define them. When updating a variable, you don't need to define the type, but any value you assign to it will try and assume its originally defined type. For example, if you define a number [int]$age = 3 and then elsewhere in your code you try and update the value to $age = "old", this will throw a conversion error as shown in the following:

```
Line |
   2 |    $age = "old"
     |    ~~~~~~~~~~~~~
     | Cannot convert value "old" to type "System.Int32". Error: "Input
       string was not in a correct format."
```

To update a value, simply assign a new one of the same type to the variable:

```
$age = 38
$age = 83
$age = 23
```

In the preceding example, the final value of $age is 23.

Accessing Variables

To access the value of a variable, simply use its name within your script. Let's set up a variable and return its value:

```
[int]$age = 37
$age
```

You can see, by typing this code into the Visual Studio Code PowerShell terminal window, that simply calling $age will return its value as shown in Figure 3-1.

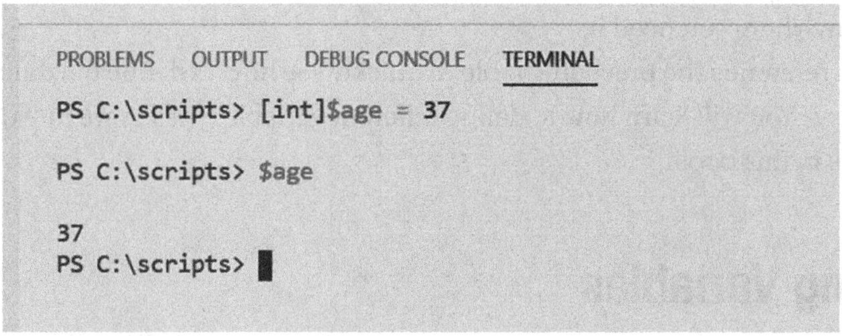

Figure 3-1. *Accessing variable values*

We can extend this example and combine the age variable into a line of code that writes a string to the console as shown in Figure 3-2:

```
Write-Host "It's my birthday and i'm " $age
```

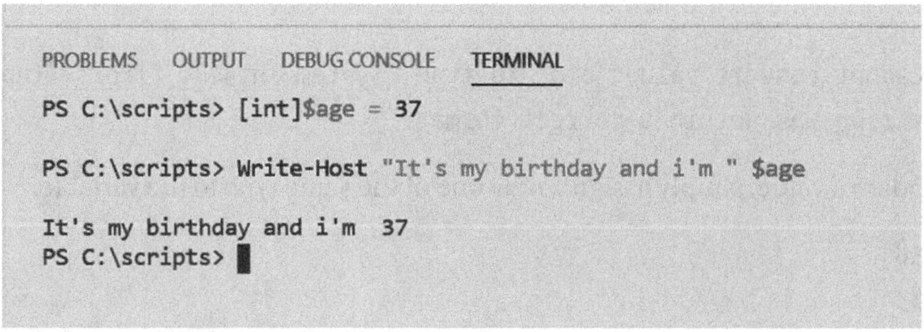

Figure 3-2. *Write-Host cmdlet*

Variable Scope

Within the PowerShell language, there is the idea of a variable scope. The reason and benefits of this behavior will become clearer as you write more complicated scripts.

The scopes are defined as follows:

Scope	
Local	Variables are visible from within the current script, function, or class only.
Global	Variables can be seen anywhere within your current PowerShell session.
Script	The scope is created when a script is run.
Private	Variables cannot be seen from another scope.

By default, when you create a variable, its scope is set to local. This means it can only be seen from where it was created. If you create a variable at the top of your script, it will be visible within the script and from any function you define. If however you create a variable within a function, it will not be accessible from outside of it.

Global Variables

Global variables can be very useful in large scripts that use lots of different classes or modules. In some of the games we will work on in this book, we will use global variables to store game characters, level objects, and high scores. Global variables make it easier to keep track of important values or objects.

Global variables are prefixed with $global: followed by their name. For example, if we were creating a game and wanted to store the position on the screen as global variables, we might do this:

```
#Player position
[int]$global:xPosition = 4
[int]$global:yPosition = 3
```

Now these two global number variables can be used anywhere within your code without having to worry about the scope restrictions. If you need to return the value of a global variable, call it like this:

```
$global:xPosition
```

Typing this code directly into the terminal should result in the xPosition variable outputting the number 4 to the console as demonstrated in Figure 3-3.

```
PROBLEMS    OUTPUT    DEBUG CONSOLE    TERMINAL

PS C:\scripts> #Player position

PS C:\scripts> [int]$global:xPosition = 4

PS C:\scripts> [int]$global:yPosition = 3

PS C:\scripts> $global:xPosition

4
PS C:\scripts> █
```

Figure 3-3. *Global variables*

Conclusion

Global variables are very useful, but don't get into the habit of using them all of the time without good reason. Most of the time, you will want to create variables for a quick calculation and then throw them away. There is no point creating everything as global since it overcomplicates your code and makes debugging a lot harder. Having to debug code at the end of your script and having to jump back to the top to try and find a global variable is time consuming and unnecessary. Use global variables for tracking important high-level values.

CHAPTER 4

Conditional Statements

Conditional statements are used in code to compare variables or the result from several variables used in a sum or calculation. Conditional statements are used to do different things in your code depending on the values of variables. For example, if your script asks the player in a game if they want to walk into the left room or the right, you would read some input from the keyboard and then see what the player has typed. If they type "left," then you will use a conditional statement to check if the input string variable equals "left." If it does, then your code will jump to the code that defines what happens in the room to the left. If the input equals "right," then the conditional statement will run the code that deals with what happens in the right-hand room. Using conditional statements essentially controls the flow of your code, what happens next when certain conditions are met.

There are a couple of common ways to write conditional statements, and each has its own way of comparing values, so let's take a look.

I've bundled the code listed in this chapter into one file rather than having lots of small files to make it easy for you to try each of the examples by highlighting the code and choosing "Run Selection" within Visual Studio Code.

```
# If the values in the if statement are equal then the result of the
  statement results in a true condition.
# If a statement results in a true condition then the code within the {}
  brackets is run.
if (4 -eq 4) {
    Write-Host "4 is equal to 4"
}

if ("hello" -eq "hello") {
    Write-Host "Both strings are equal to each other"
}
```

© Ian Waters 2021
I. Waters, *PowerShell for Beginners*, https://doi.org/10.1007/978-1-4842-7064-6_4

```
# If you change the value of one of the variables they won't equal each
  other so the else clause will run.
[int]$x = 10
[int]$y = 10

if ($x -eq $y) {
    Write-Host "the x and y variables are equal to each other"
}
else {
    Write-Host "The x and y variables are NOT equal to each other"
}

# Is "Ian" equal to "Ian"? yes they are so the result is true and code
  within the if statement runs.
$yourName = "Ian"

if ($yourName -eq "Ian") {
    Write-Host "Hay my name is Ian too!"
}
else {
    Write-Host "Hi $yourName, nice to meet you!"
}

# An example of reading input from the console and using an if, elseif,
  else statements.
# Using just this code you can expand it to write your own text based
  adventure game in PowerShell!
#Variables
[string]$playerInput = ""

#Get input from player
$playerInput = Read-Host -Prompt "You walk into a room with two doorways.
One to the left and one to the right. Type 'left' or 'Right' to walk
through one of the doors."

if ($playerInput -eq "left") {
    Write-Host "Player typed left"
}
```

```
elseif ($playerInput -eq "right") {
    Write-Host "Player typed right"
}
else {
    Write-Host "Player typed something we didn't understand"
}

# Comparison Operators

# -eq Equals.
if (5 -eq 5) {
    #5 is equal to 5
}

# -ne Not equals.
if (3 -ne 4) {
    #3 is not equal to 4
}

# -gt Greater than.
if (4 -gt 2) {
    #4 is greater than 2
}

# -ge Greater than or equal.
if (2 -ge 1) {
    #2 is greater than or equal to 1
}

# -lt Less than.
if (1 -lt 2) {
    #1 is less than 1
}

# -le Less than or equal.
if (1 -le 2) {
    #1 is less than or equal to 2
}
```

```
# -like Results in a true condition when a string matches based on a
  wildcard character *.
# The string "hello*" says if this string matches the other by starting
  with the word hello followed by any other words.
# If we used "*hello*" it would mean result in true if hellow appears in
  the other string because we are using a wildcard at the start and end.
if ("hello how are you?" -like "hello*") {
    #use a wildcard character * to match strings
}

# -notlike    Results in a true condition when two strings don't match.
if ("HELLO" -notlike "BYE") {
    #HELLO is not like BYE
}

# -match      Results in true when a string matches a regex pattern. In its
             simplest form it can be used to check if a word or character
             exists in a string. Its well worth reading more on regex
             patterns as we wont be using many of these in the exapmples in
             this book.
if ("HELLO" -match "H") {
    #H exists in the
    string "HELLO"
}

# -notmatch  Results in true when a string doesn't match a regex pattern.
if ("HELLO" -notmatch "A") {
    #A does not match in the
    string "HELLO"
}

# -contains  Results in true when a value is found within another
             collection.
$list = @(1, 2, 3, 4, 5)
if ($list -contains 3) {
    #the list does contain a 3
}
```

```
# -notcontains      Results in true when a value is not found within a
                    collection.
$list = @(1, 2, 3, 4, 5)
if ($list -notcontains 8) {
    #$list does not contain 8
}

# -in               Results in true when a value is found in a collection.
$list = @(1, 2, 3, 4, 5)
if (3 -in $list) {
    #the list does contain a 3
}

# -notin            Results in true when a value is not found in a collection.
$list = @(1, 2, 3, 4, 5)
if (6 -notin $list) {
    #6 is not in the list
}

# -is               Results in true when a variable or value matches the
                    specified type.
$var = "This is a string"
if ($var -is [string]) {
    #The variable is a string
}

# -isnot            Results in true when a variable or value is not equal
                    to the specified type.
$var = "This is a string"
if ($var -isnot [bool]) {
    #The variable is a string and not a Boolean value so results in true.
}

# Switch Statements

# In this example we set up a number variables and pass it into the switch.
# On each line we place the value to compare against.
# In this case the numbers 1 and 2 and after each value we use {} brackets
  to define the code to run when that value matches.
```

```
[int]$number = 2
switch ($number) {
    1 { "The number is one" }
    2 { "The number is two" }
    default { "I dont know what the number is" }
}

# This is to show within each clause you can run multiple lines of code not
  just one.
# The final clause is default which will run if none of the values match.
[string]$favouriteColour = "Blue"
switch ($favouriteColour) {
    "Red" {
        "Your favourite colour is Red"
        "I like red too."
    }

    "Blue" {
        "Your favourite colour is Blue"
        "I like Blue too."
    }

    default { "I dont recognise that colour" }
}
```

if Statements

The most common conditional statement is the if statement. If this happens, then do this; else, do this; else, do this; and so on.

Let's look at a couple of simple examples where we compare values or variables to each other and see if they are equal. If they are equal, then the statement results in a true condition. If a statement results in a true condition, then the code within the {} brackets is run:

```
if (4 -eq 4) {
 Write-Host "4 is equal to 4"
}
```

```
if ("hello" -eq "hello") {
 Write-Host "Both strings are equal to each other"
}
```

As shown in Figure 4-1, when you run the script, you can see that both if statements equal to true since 4 equals 4 and the string "hello" equals the other string "hello", so the code within the if statements executes. The output from the Write-Host cmdlet gets written out to the Visual Studio Code terminal.

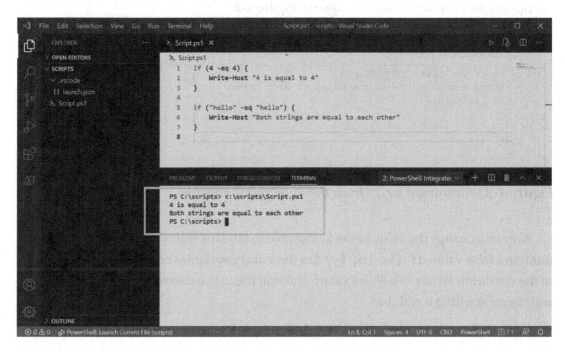

Figure 4-1. *Running a script directly from the terminal window*

From now on, I will run all scripts from a Script.ps1 file directly within a PowerShell console. This will save space in the book and focus attention on the output of various scripts.

Let's introduce the else clause after the if statement. An else can be used to catch any results that don't match the if condition. In the following example, we set up two number variables and compare them. If they match, the if statement results in true, and the code within the {} brackets runs. If you change the value of one of the variables, they won't equal each other, so the else clause will run:

```
[int]$x = 10
[int]$y = 10
```

```
if ($x -eq $y) {
 Write-Host "the x and y variables are equal to each other"
}
else {
 Write-Host "The x and y variables are NOT equal to each other"
}
```

Within the PowerShell console you can run the script file directly by typing .\script.ps1 and pressing enter as shown in Figure 4-2.

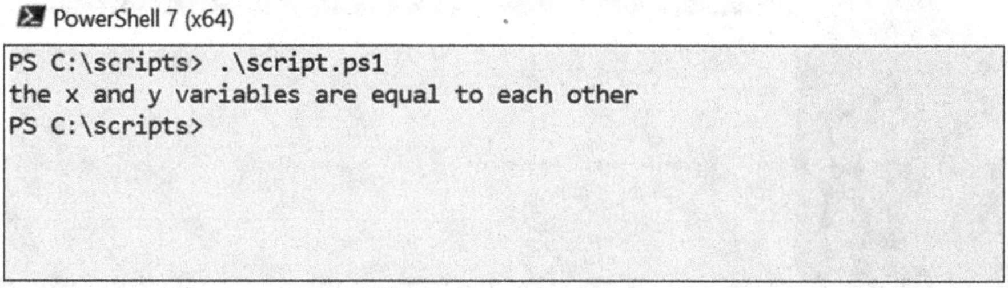

Figure 4-2. *Running a script from the PowerShell console*

Now let's change the value of the $y variable to 20. This will make the if statement result in a false value. if ($x -eq $y) Are the x and y variables equal? No, they aren't, so the condition results in a $false value. This will mean the else statement will trigger and the code within it will run:

```
[int]$x = 10
[int]$y = 20
```

```
if ($x -eq $y) {
 Write-Host "the x and y variables are equal to each other"
}
else {
 Write-Host "The x and y variables are NOT equal to each other"
}
```

Just as expected, $x and $y are not equal to each other, so the else clause is triggered and the code within it runs. We can verify that by running the script, and the output is as expected in Figure 4-3.

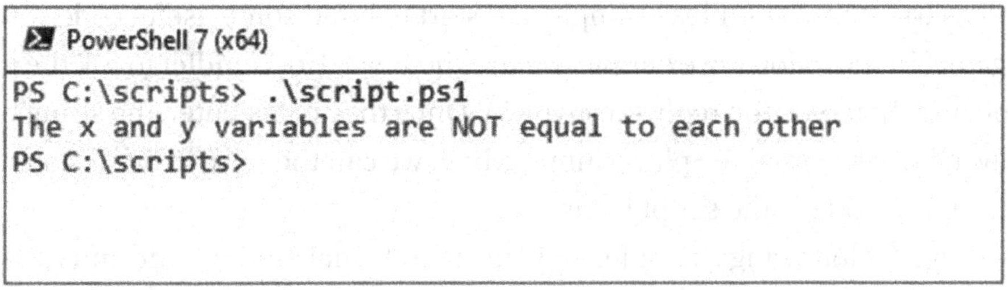

```
PowerShell 7 (x64)
PS C:\scripts> .\script.ps1
The x and y variables are NOT equal to each other
PS C:\scripts>
```

Figure 4-3. *Testing if x and y int variables are equal to each other*

In the following example, you will see that you can mix variables and actual values within an if statement. Here, we compare a variable against a string to see if they match. They are in fact both string types, the variable and the typed text. Since they are the same, the if statement results in a true condition. Are "Ian" and "Ian" equal? Yes, they are, so the result is true and the code within the if statement runs:

```
$yourName = "Ian"

if ($yourName -eq "Ian") {
 Write-Host "Hay my name is Ian too!"
}
else {
 Write-Host "Hi $yourName, nice to meet you!"
}
```

If we run the code, we can see that the variable $yourName is indeed equal to "Ian", which results in the condition being true, so the code within the if clause runs and outputs "Hay my name is Ian too!" as shown in Figure 4-4.

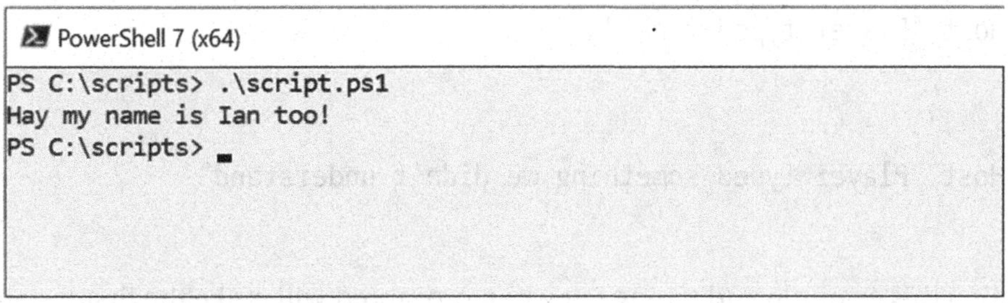

```
PowerShell 7 (x64)
PS C:\scripts> .\script.ps1
Hay my name is Ian too!
PS C:\scripts>
```

Figure 4-4. *Testing if two strings are the same*

Now let's try a more complex example and start to build some useful code you can use in a game. In the following example, we use the Read-Host cmdlet to ask the user a question and then read the reply they type in. Once they press Enter, the string typed will be saved into the variable $playerInput, which we can then use in our if statement to determine which code in the script is run.

Try writing the following example out yourself in Visual Studio Code and run it. Change the value of the $playerInput variable and see how each section of code runs. Notice the use of if and else if clauses. You can add as many else if conditions as you want, but the first is always an if statement. Also notice at the end there is an else statement. You can end an if statement with an else when you want to run code that fails to get triggered by any of the if or else if conditions.

Within each condition, you will notice the -eq. This is called a comparison operator, and -eq means "equals." There are a number of comparison operators you can use, which we will take a look at next, but for now try out the following code example and experiment with if else statements to get familiar with how they work:

```
#Variables
[string]$playerInput = ""

#Get input from player
$playerInput = Read-Host -Prompt "You walk into a room with two doorways.
One to the left and one to the right. Type 'left' or 'Right' to walk
through one of the doors."

if ($playerInput -eq "left") {
 Write-Host "Player typed left"
}
elseif ($playerInput -eq "right") {
 Write-Host "Player typed right"
}
else {
 Write-Host "Player typed something we didn't understand"
}
```

Running this example and typing left when prompted will make the first if statement result in true, which then runs the code within it as shown in Figure 4-5.

```
PowerShell 7 (x64)                                                          —    □    ×
PS C:\scripts> .\script.ps1
You walk into a room with two doorways. One to the left and one to the right. Type 'left' or 'Right' to walk through one
 of the doors.: left
Player typed left
PS C:\scripts>
```

Figure 4-5. *Using the Read-Host cmdlet to capture typed input*

Comparison Operators

Comparison operators are used to compare variables or the result of a calculation to determine what to do next in your script. You can compare numbers to see if one is greater than or less than the other. You can see if two string variables exactly match including the upper- and lowercase letters, or you can ignore the case of letters. There are a number of comparison operators to use in your scripts when comparing variables or the results of calculations.

-eq	Equals	if (5 -eq 5) {
		  #5 is equal to 5
		}

-ne	Not equals	if (3 -ne 4) {
		  #3 is not equal to 4
		}

-gt	Greater than	if (4 -gt 2) {
		  #4 is greater than 2
		}

-ge	Greater than or equal to	if (2 -ge 1) {
		  #2 is greater than or equal
		  to 1
		}

-lt	Less than	if (1 -lt 2) {
		  #1 is less than 1
		}

(continued)

51

| -le | Less than or equal to | ```
if (1 -le 2) {
    #1 is less than or equal to 2
}
``` |
| -like | Results in a true condition when a string matches based on a wildcard character * <br> Using the string "hello*", it means a string matches the other by starting with the word hello followed by any other words. <br> If we used "*hello*", it would result in true if hello appears in the other string because we are using a wildcard at the start and end. | ```
if ("hello how are you?" -like
"hello*") {
    #use a wildcard character *
    to match strings
}
``` |
| -notlike | Results in a true condition when two strings don't match | ```
if ("HELLO" -notlike "BYE") {
    #HELLO is not like BYE
}
``` |
| -match | Results in true when a string matches a regex pattern. In its simplest form, it can be used to check if a word or character exists in a string. It's well worth reading more on regex patterns as we won't be using many of these in the examples in this book | ```
if ("HELLO" -match "H") {
    #H exists in the string
    "HELLO"
}
``` |
| -notmatch | Results in true when a string doesn't match a regex pattern | ```
if ("HELLO" -notmatch "A") {
    #A does not match in the
    string "HELLO"
}
``` |
| -contains | Results in true when a value is found within a collection | ```
$list = @(1, 2, 3, 4, 5)

if ($list -contains 3) {
    #the list does contain a 3
}
``` |

(continued)

-notcontains	Results in true when a value is not found within a collection	`$list = @(1, 2, 3, 4, 5)`
		
		`if ($list -notcontains 8) {`
		`    #$list does not contain 8`
		`}`

-in	Results in true when a value is found in a collection	`$list = @(1, 2, 3, 4, 5)`
		
		`if (3 -in $list) {`
		`    #the list does contain a 3`
		`}`

-notin	Results in true when a value is not found in a collection	`$list = @(1, 2, 3, 4, 5)`
		
		`if (6 -notin $list) {`
		`    #6 is not in the list`
		`}`

-is	Results in true when a variable or value matches the specified type	`$var = "This is a string"`
		
		`if ($var -is [string]) {`
		`    #The variable is a string`
		`}`

-isnot	Results in true when a variable or value is not equal to the specified type	`$var = "This is a string"`
		
		`if ($var -isnot [bool]) {`
		`    #The variable is a string and`
		`    not a Boolean value so`
		`    results in true.`
		`}`

Switch Statement

A switch statement is a useful way of checking a value or variable against a number of different values quickly. To set up a switch, you pass in the variable and compare against the values you define. If the variable matches, then the code in that section will run. Similar to the if statement's else clause, in a switch, you can code a section that will run if none of the values match by using the default clause. The default clause is the default action if none of the other sections match.

In this example, we set up a number variable and pass it into the switch. On each line, we place the value to compare against, in this case, the numbers 1 and 2. After each value, we use {} brackets to define the code to run when that value matches:

```
[int]$number = 2
switch ($number) {
 1 { "The number is one" }
 2 { "The number is two" }
 default { "I dont know what the number is" }
}
```

If you run this code, the $number variable matches against number 2, and that section of code runs as shown in Figure 4-6.

```
PowerShell 7 (x64)
PS C:\scripts> .\script.ps1
The number is two
PS C:\scripts>
```

Figure 4-6. *Using a switch statement with numbers*

In the following example, we define a string variable $favouriteColour and set it to "Blue". We pass in the variable to the switch and compare it against the values "Red" and "Blue". Notice in this example I move the brackets onto their own line. This is just to show that within each clause you can run multiple lines of code, not just one. The final clause is default, which will run if none of the values match:

```
[string]$favouriteColour = "Blue"
switch ($favouriteColour) {
    "Red" {
        "Your favourite colour is Red"
        "I like red too."
    }
```

```
    "Blue" {
        "Your favourite colour is Blue"
        "I like Blue too."
    }

        default { "I dont recognise that colour" }
}
```

If you run this code, the variable $favouriteColour will equal to the text "Blue", and so that section of code will run as shown in Figure 4-7.

```
PowerShell 7 (x64)
PS C:\scripts> .\script.ps1
Your favourite colour is Blue
PS C:\scripts>
```

Figure 4-7. *Using a switch statement with string variables*

Conclusion

When developing your own scripts, you will use conditional statements a lot, but which type you use is a matter of preference and need. I will typically default to if statements because they are more versatile in being able to compare values in different ways. When I need to compare one variable against a larger number of values and only run small amounts of code in each, then a switch statement is great to keep code lean and mean. Experiment with the code in this chapter as much as possible especially the if statements and comparison operators. See how each one works and get familiar with using them to compare different values. As I said earlier, you will be using them a lot, so being comfortable writing out if statements and comparing values in different ways will make you a better coder.

CHAPTER 5

Loops

Loops are another really useful tool when writing scripts. Loops are great for running code multiple times based on the value of a variable. They can be useful for checking values in a list of variables.

I've bundled the code listed in this chapter into one file to make it easy for you to try each of the examples by highlighting the code and choosing "Run Selection" within Visual Studio Code.

```
# Each time around the loop the code in the brackets will run while
  $counter is less than than $repeat.
# Each time around the loop the ++ symbols tell the variable to increment
  by one each time.
[int]$repeat = 5

for ($counter = 0; $counter -lt $repeat; $counter++) {
    Write-Host "hello"
}

# The while loop will continue until $counter is less than (-lt) the value
  5 held in the $repeat variable.
[int]$repeat = 5
[int]$counter = 0

while ($counter -lt $repeat) {
    Write-Host "hello"
    $counter++
}
```

© Ian Waters 2021
I. Waters, *PowerShell for Beginners*, https://doi.org/10.1007/978-1-4842-7064-6_5

```
# Do While Loop is a variant of the while loop except the code is executed
  before the condition is checked to see if it repeats.
[int]$repeat = 5
[int]$counter = 0
do {
    Write-Host "hello"
    $counter++
}
while ($counter -lt $repeat)

# ForEach Loop
# Each time around the loop the $character variable becomes the next
  character in the list until there are no characters left.
[string]$stringOfCharacters = "PowerShell for Beginners"

foreach ($character in $stringOfCharacters.ToCharArray()) {
    Write-Host $character
}

# ForEach-Object loops
[string]$stringOfCharacters = "PowerShell for Beginners"
$stringOfCharacters.ToCharArray() | ForEach-Object { Write-Host "$_" }
```

For Loops

For loops are great for repeating a section of code multiple times. Let's start with a basic example, which will display "hello" to the screen based on the value we give the $repeat variable.

A for loop is made up of three sections separated by a semicolon:

- The first section defines the number variable, and here we call it counter and set it to zero.

- The second section is a stop condition. If the result of the condition is true, the loop keeps repeating; and if it is false, the loop stops. Here we say if $counter is less than $repeat, then loop again. The stop condition is where you say how long to keep repeating the loop.

- The final section is used to change the first variable each time around the loop. Most of the time you will want to increase it by one, but you may want to increase it by two or any other value you want.

A quick tip here is that if you ever want to increase an [int] number by one, you can put ++ on the end of it. In this example, $counter will increase by one each time it goes around the loop.

Let's take a look at a simple example, which outputs "hello" to the console for a set number of times.

First, we set up an integer (number) variable and set it to 5. We will use this in the for loop to set the number of times to go round the loop.

In the for loop, we set a variable $counter to 0. Next, we specify a condition that determines if the loop continues round or not. In this case, we say repeat the loop if $counter is less than the $repeat variable. If this evaluates to true, then continue round the loop.

Here we use a -lt comparison operator, but you could also use the -lte operator if you want the loop to repeat until both $counter and $repeat are equal to each other.

In this case, we set $counter to 0, so to write "hello" five times to the screen, we need to use the -lt operator to ensure hello is not repeated six times since we start at 0.

Using the less than -lt operator will result in $counter reaching the number 4 before the loop stops; this results in hello being displayed five times because we start at 0:

0 1 2 3 4

If we used the less than or equal to operator -lte, $counter would get incremented until it's equal to 5. This will print out six hello's to the console because it starts at 0:

0 1 2 3 4 5

Play around with different comparison operators in this example to get more familiar with how to use them.

Finally, we update the $counter variable and increase it by one each time round the loop using ++, which means increase the variable by 1. The loop continues as long as $counter is less than $repeat using the -lt comparison operator.

Each time around the loop, the code in the brackets will run while $counter is less than $repeat:

```
[int]$repeat = 5

for ($counter = 0; $counter -lt $repeat; $counter++) {
    Write-Host "hello"
}
```

Running the code results in hello being written to the console five times because the variable $counter gets set to 0 and then gets increased by one until the condition equals false as shown in Figure 5-1.

```
 PowerShell 7 (x64)

PS C:\scripts> .\script.ps1
hello
hello
hello
hello
hello
PS C:\scripts>
```

Figure 5-1. Using a for loop

While Loops

While loops are used to repeat a section of code as long as a condition equals true. Using the previous for loop example, we can write the same code using a while loop. First, we set the integer variables. We set $repeat to 5 and $counter to 0 and then use a while loop to check for the condition ($counter -lt $repeat) to equate to the value $true. Inside the loop, we write "hello" to the console and increment the $counter variable by one each time.

The while loop will continue as long as $counter is less than (-lt) the value 5 held in the $repeat variable:

```
[int]$repeat  = 5
[int]$counter = 0

while ($counter -lt $repeat) {
    Write-Host "hello"
    $counter++
}
```

Do While Loops

Do while loops can be used in the same way as a for loop, but they use more lines of code. Here is the same script written out as a do while loop. You can see that the code runs and then the condition is checked at the end in the while statement, but setting up the variables and incrementing the counter is done separately the same way we did when using the while loop. This is just a variant, except the code is executed before the condition is checked to see if it repeats:

```
[int]$repeat = 5
[int]$counter = 0

do {
    Write-Host "hello"
    $counter++
}
while ($counter -lt $repeat)
```

If you run this example, you can see the output results in hello being written out to the console five times, the same result we've seen using a for and while loop just written a different way. When writing your own code, use whichever loop type you feel comfortable using. Over time you will get a feel for which type of loop is appropriate to use in each situation. Running the script results in 6 hello's being written to the console until the while condition equals false as shown in Figure 5-2.

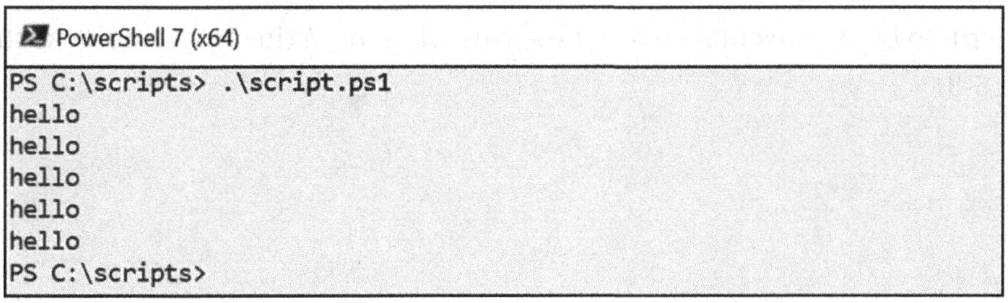

```
PowerShell 7 (x64)
PS C:\scripts> .\script.ps1
hello
hello
hello
hello
hello
PS C:\scripts>
```

Figure 5-2. *Using a do while loop*

Do while loops can be used when you want to stop looping when two values meet the while condition, so they are not just for comparing number values, but also if you want to compare two string variables and repeat the code until they result in a true condition. If you don't need a counter in your loop to keep track of the number of times it's run, then a do while is a good choice. Also remember do while loops will run the code in the loop at least once, whereas while or for loops might never run at all if the conditions are not met.

Foreach Loops

Foreach loops are great for looping through lists or collections of variables. A foreach loop is made up of a variable that will become each object in a list of objects. You will learn about lists or, as they are called in PowerShell, arrays; but in this example, we define a string variable and then convert it to an array of characters. The foreach loop will then loop through this list of characters. Each time around the loop, the $character variable becomes the next character in the list until there are no characters left.

```
[string]$stringOfCharacters = "PowerShell for Beginners"

foreach ($character in $stringOfCharacters.ToCharArray()) {
    Write-Host $character
}
```

Running this code results in the $character variable being set to each character in the string "PowerShell for Beginners". Each time round the loop, the next character in the string is written out to the console on a new line using the Write-Host cmdlet as shown in Figure 5-3.

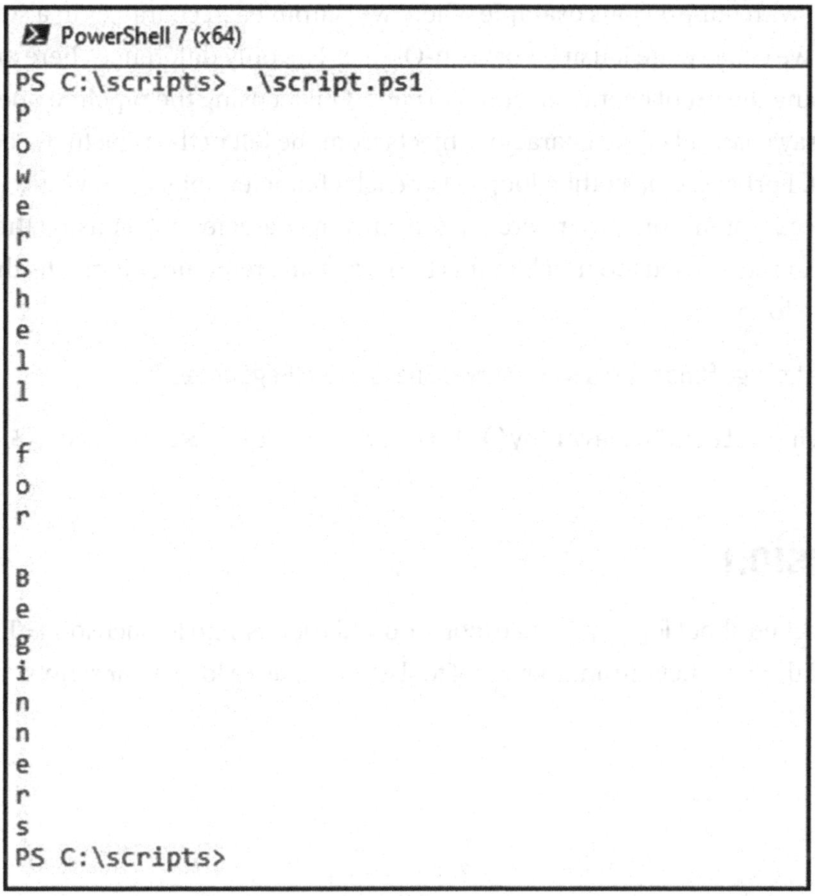

```
PowerShell 7 (x64)

PS C:\scripts> .\script.ps1
P
o
w
e
r
S
h
e
l
l

f
o
r

B
e
g
i
n
n
e
r
s
PS C:\scripts>
```

Figure 5-3. *Using a for each loop*

Within a game, you could use a foreach loop to control each character in the game, looping through all of the characters and making them move a little bit at a time. In a networking script, you could generate a list of computers on the network and then use a foreach loop to perform some action on each computer object in the list.

ForEach-Object Loops

ForEach-Object loops work in a similar way to foreach loops except they require the input to be piped to them. ForEach-Object will then loop through each object passed to it and run the code specified within the {} brackets.

Sticking with our previous example where we output each character in a string to the screen, we can rewrite it using ForEach-Object. The only differences here are that we are passing the list of characters into ForEach-Object using the pipeline operator |, which just says pass all of the character objects from the left of the pipe to the command on the right. ForEach-Object then loops over each character object and writes it out to the console except this time we reference the current character object using the variable $_. You won't see $_ used too much in this book, but just remember it means the current object in the loop:

```
[string]$stringOfCharacters = "PowerShell for Beginners"

$stringOfCharacters.ToCharArray() | ForEach-Object { Write-Host "$_" }
```

Conclusion

You have learned about for loops, while loops, do while loops, and foreach loops. Experiment with each of these as they are another set of tools you will use a lot in your scripts.

CHAPTER 6

Arrays

Arrays are a list of objects such as strings and numbers, but they can contain any type of object you set up. Arrays can even contain a mix of different types of objects making them perfect for storing lots of values or objects in your scripts that need to be looped through or referred to later. Arrays and other types of lists in PowerShell are often referred to as collections, "a collection of objects."

There are two common types of arrays you will see in PowerShell scripts. The first is the [Array] object, which is easy to use and of a fixed size. Second, we can also utilize the .Net class and create an ArrayList.

Remember from Chapter 1, "Terminology" section, PowerShell is built on top of .Net and .Net contains a vast number of prebuilt objects and code we can utilize in our PowerShell scripts. Many of these prebuilt objects offer improved performance and abilities we can leverage in our code to improve it.

Both share common properties and methods, but array lists are faster and a little more flexible, thanks to the power of .Net. We will take a look at Array first and then look at creating an ArrayList object and see what the main differences are. Further on in the book, you will see my preference to use an ArrayList due to speed and flexibility, but it's good for you to see both being used in the following examples.

I've bundled the code listed in this chapter into one file to make it easy for you to try each of the examples by highlighting the code and choosing "Run Selection" within Visual Studio Code.

```
# You can define an array by using the type Array and setting its initial
  value to @().
# This means create an empty array but you can also initiliase the array
  with an initial set of values.
[Array]$myArray = @(1, 2, 3, 5, 6, 7, 8, 9, 10)
$myArray
```

© Ian Waters 2021
I. Waters, *PowerShell for Beginners*, https://doi.org/10.1007/978-1-4842-7064-6_6

```
# Filling an array with strings.
[Array]$names = @("Ian", "Steve", "Rebecca", "Claire")
$names

# Creating a mixed object array.
[Array]$mixedArray = @("Ian", 4, 45.6, "Rebecca", 'A')
$mixedArray

# Accessing array properties such as count (number of itmes in the array).
[Array]$myArray = @(1, 2, 3, 4, 6, 7, 8, 9, 10)
Write-Host "Count:" $myArray.Count
Write-Host "IsFixedSize:" $myArray.IsFixedSize

# Accessing an entry in the Array. Remember the array starts at 0 where the
    first item is located.
[System.Collections.ArrayList]$names = @("Ian", "Steve", "Rebecca",
"Claire")
Write-Host "Object from index 2:" $names[2]

# Looping through an array using a for loop.
[System.Collections.ArrayList]$names = @("Ian", "Steve", "Rebecca", "Claire")
for ($index = 0; $index -lt $names.Count; $index++) {
    Write-Host "Object from index $index" $names[$index]
}

# Looping through an array using a foreach loop.
[System.Collections.ArrayList]$names = @("Ian", "Steve", "Rebecca",
"Claire")
foreach ($var in $names) {
    Write-Host "Current object in the array:" $var
}

# Removing an item from an array.
[System.Collections.ArrayList]$names = @("Ian", "Steve", "Rebecca", "Claire")
Write-Host "Original list of names:"
$names
$names.Remove("Claire")
Write-Host "New list of names:"
$names
```

```
# Removing an entry from the array using the index position in the array.
[System.Collections.ArrayList]$names = @("Ian", "Steve", "Rebecca",
"Claire")
Write-Host "Original list of names:"
$names
$names.RemoveAt(0)
Write-Host "New list of names:"
$names
```

Initializing an Array

You can define an array by using the type Array and setting its initial value to @(). This means create an empty array, but you can also initialize the array with an initial set of values.

```
[Array]$myArray = @(1, 2, 3, 5, 6, 7, 8, 9, 10)
$myArray
```

Running this code will simply output each object stored in the array to the console as shown here in Figure 6-1.

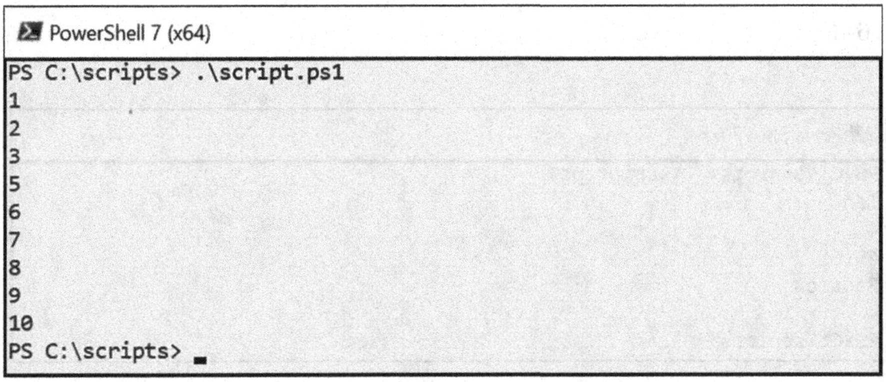

Figure 6-1. *Initializing an array with number values*

Next, let's create an array called $names and fill it up with a few names and output the contents to the console:

```
[Array]$names = @("Ian", "Steve", "Rebecca", "Claire")
$names
```

As we've seen previously, the contents of the $names array are output to the console shown here in Figure 6-2.

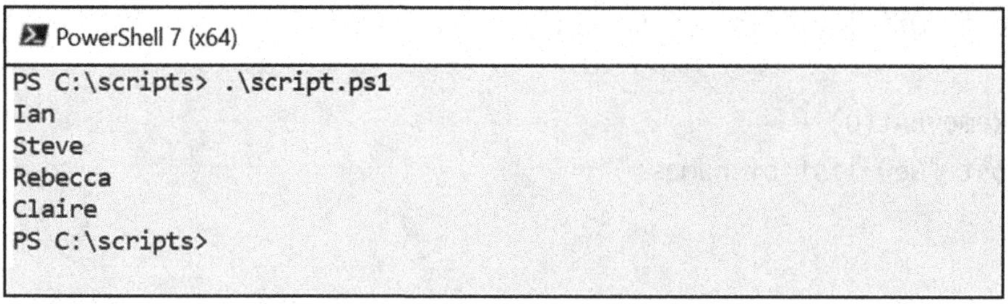

```
PowerShell 7 (x64)
PS C:\scripts> .\script.ps1
Ian
Steve
Rebecca
Claire
PS C:\scripts>
```

Figure 6-2. *Initializing an array with string values*

Since an array is simply a collection of objects, that means we can add different types of objects to it. In the following code example and in the output shown in Figure 6-3, we can fill an array with different object types. We will fill $mixedArray with a string, an integer, a double, another string, and a single-character object:

```
[Array]$mixedArray = @("Ian", 4, 45.6, "Rebecca", 'A')
$mixedArray
```

If we run this code example, we can see all objects output to the console shown here in Figure 6-3.

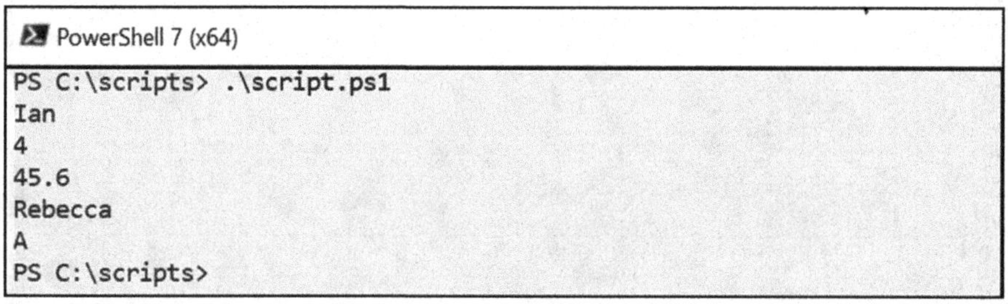

```
PowerShell 7 (x64)
PS C:\scripts> .\script.ps1
Ian
4
45.6
Rebecca
A
PS C:\scripts>
```

Figure 6-3. *Initializing a mixed–object type array*

Array Properties and Methods

An Array object has many properties and methods we can use to work with the objects stored in it. Properties are values within an array we can access that tell us something useful about it such as the number of stored objects and length. Within an array, we can use the following properties:

.Count – Number of objects stored in the array

.IsFixedSize – Whether items can be removed from or added to the array

```
[Array]$myArray = @(1, 2, 3, 4, 6, 7, 8, 9, 10)
Write-Host "Count:" $myArray.Count
Write-Host "IsFixedSize:" $myArray.IsFixedSize
```

Running this code, we can see the values of the .Count and .IsFixedSize properties as shown in Figure 6-4.

```
 PowerShell 7 (x64)
PS C:\scripts> .\script.ps1
Count: 9
IsFixedSize: True
PS C:\scripts>
```

Figure 6-4. *Accessing array details*

[Array] and [System.collections.ArrayList] objects have a set of methods we can use to add and remove items to and from them. [Array] objects are of a fixed size, so although the methods are available, you can't actually add or remove items to or from them as you will see later in this chapter.

- `Int .Add( System.Object )` – Adds the new object to the ArrayList and returns the new length of the list.

- `Void .Clear()` – Clears all objects from the ArrayList but keeps its size.

- `Bool .Contains( System.Object )` – Used to check if a collection contains a specified object.

- `Void .Insert( int, System.Object )` – Used to place a new object at a specified position.

- `Void .Remove( System.Object )` – Used to remove a matching object from the list.

- `Void .RemoveAt( int )` – Used to remove the object at the specified position. Remember the first position in a list is zero.

Accessing Values in an Array

Accessing values in an Array object or ArrayList can be done by specifying the index within the collection and reading the value.

Let's take a look at our names example from earlier. Here we have an ArrayList object that contains four string objects. Objects in the collection can be selected by specifying their index in the list starting from 0:

- Index 0 would refer to "Ian".

- Index 1 would refer to "Steve".

Many people learning programming forget this and assume the first item in a list starts at 1, but no, the first entry in a list starts at 0.

```
[System.Collections.ArrayList]$names = @("Ian", "Steve", "Rebecca", "Claire")

Write-Host "Object from index 2:" $names[2]
```

Running this code example, we can see in Figure 6-5 that the object at index 2 in the $names array variable returns "Rebecca". Remember that arrays start at index position 0, so the number 2 is really referencing the third item in the list.

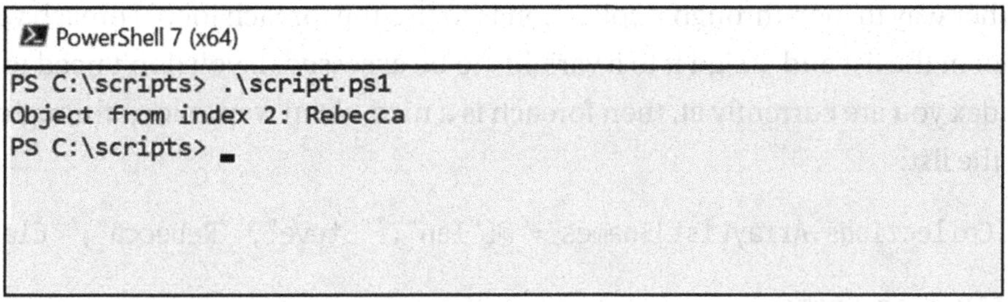

```
PowerShell 7 (x64)
PS C:\scripts> .\script.ps1
Object from index 2: Rebecca
PS C:\scripts>
```

Figure 6-5. *Accessing objects in an array*

We can also reference a position in an array by using a number variable. We could loop through all of the values in the array by using a for loop and use the counter variable as a way to specify the object to return:

```
[System.Collections.ArrayList]$names = @("Ian", "Steve", "Rebecca",
"Claire")

for($index = 0;$index -lt $names.Count;$index++)
{
    Write-Host "Object from index $index" $names[$index]
}
```

You can see in Figure 6-6 the for loop increments $index from 0 until it's equal to .Count, which represents the number of objects in the array. $index is used to reference each position in the array from 0 to 3 in this example, which is a total of four objects.

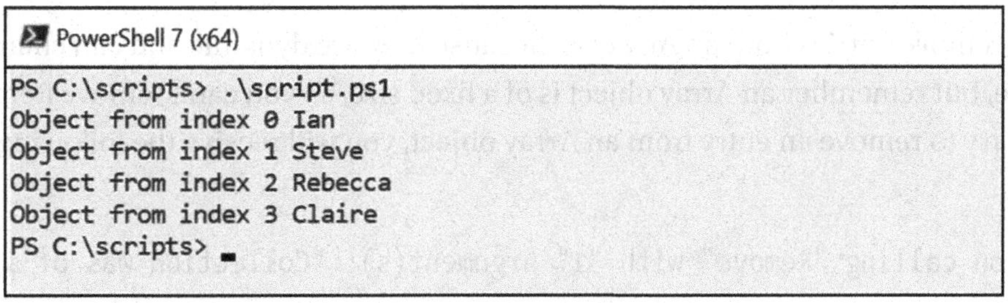

```
PowerShell 7 (x64)
PS C:\scripts> .\script.ps1
Object from index 0 Ian
Object from index 1 Steve
Object from index 2 Rebecca
Object from index 3 Claire
PS C:\scripts>
```

Figure 6-6. *Using a for loop to access objects in an array*

Another way to loop through a collection is to use the foreach loop. Foreach will visit every item in the list and assign it to a variable to be accessed. If you don't need to know which index you are currently at, then foreach is a nice, clean way to loop through all items in the list:

```
[System.Collections.ArrayList]$names = @("Ian", "Steve", "Rebecca", "Claire")

foreach($var in $names)
{
    Write-Host "Current object in the array:" $var
}
```

If we run this code example, we can see all objects output to the console shown here in Figure 6-7.

```
PowerShell 7 (x64)
PS C:\scripts> .\script.ps1
Current object in the array: Ian
Current object in the array: Steve
Current object in the array: Rebecca
Current object in the array: Claire
PS C:\scripts>
```

Figure 6-7. *Using a foreach loop to access string objects in an array*

Removing Values from an Array

You can remove entries from an ArrayList because they are dynamic and can change their size, but remember an Array object is of a fixed size, so you can't remove items from it. If you try to remove an entry from an Array object, you will receive the following error message:

```
Exception calling "Remove" with "1" argument(s): "Collection was of a fixed
size."
```

This is one reason to get in the habit of using an ArrayList unless you know the list will never change once it's been created. An ArrayList is more flexible but at the cost of a performance hit. Using an Array object containing lots of objects will often run faster compared to an ArrayList, so bear this in mind when developing your own scripts.

Let's set up a new ArrayList, fill it with names, and remove one of the names:

```
[System.Collections.ArrayList]$names = @("Ian", "Steve", "Rebecca", "Claire")

Write-host "Original list of names:"
$names

$names.Remove("Claire")

Write-host "New list of names:"
$names
```

Running the code, we can see in Figure 6-8 that at first the array displays the full content and then the array outputs the objects again only this time without the "Claire" string object.

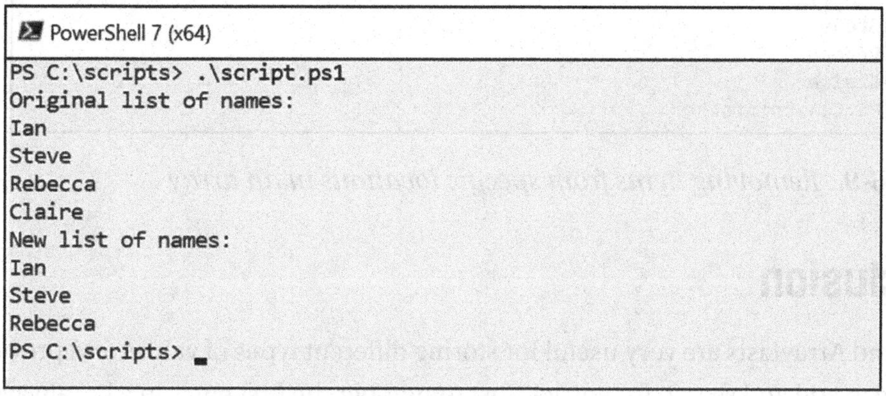

Figure 6-8. Removing items from an array

We can also remove entries from an ArrayList by using RemoveAt and specifying the index of the entry. As mentioned earlier, within all collections, the first entry's index is 0. In this example, we call RemoveAt with a 0 with the aim of removing "Ian" from the list of names:

```
[System.Collections.ArrayList]$names = @("Ian", "Steve", "Rebecca", "Claire")

Write-host "Original list of names:"
$names
```

```
$names.RemoveAt(0)
```

```
Write-host "New list of names:"
$names
```

If we run this code example, we can see all objects being output to the console and then the list displays again only this time it doesn't contain the object that was at position 0 as shown here in Figure 6-9.

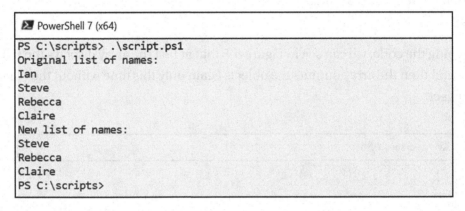

Figure 6-9. *Removing items from specific locations in an array*

Conclusion

Arrays and ArrayLists are very useful for storing different types of values and provide an easy way to add and search for entries. Just remember the first entry in a list always starts at 0 and use an ArrayList if you want to remove entries after your array has been created.

CHAPTER 7

Functions

Functions are a great way to keep code organized and easy to follow. Functions group code together to perform a specific task, which can be called from anywhere in your script. If you need to run the same block of code multiple times, you can just write it once in a function and then call that code by writing the function name. Once the script reaches that point, it will jump to the block of code in the function and run the code and then jump back to where the function was called from and continue.

You can pass variables or values to functions, and functions can even return values via an object.

Creating a Function

To create a function, simply type function followed by a name of your choice. The code within the function is grouped together by curly brackets {}. When naming a function, there are PowerShell scripting guidelines that are worth following. Names should start with a verb that denotes the function's action such as "Get," "Set," or "Show" followed by a noun, the item being acted upon. You will see this naming convention more and more as you read code examples, and it makes functions easier to read and understand.

Let's take a look at a simple function example. In this script, the PowerShell console is cleared, and then the function Show-Menu is defined. Within the function, we display a menu screen to the user. The script won't execute any code within the function until the function is called by its name, so at the end of the script, we simply call Show-Menu to run it.

© Ian Waters 2021
I. Waters, *PowerShell for Beginners*, https://doi.org/10.1007/978-1-4842-7064-6_7

```
#Beginners Guide to Functions

function Show-Menu
{
    #Display menu options
    Write-Host "------------"
    Write-Host "Menu Options"
    Write-Host "-----------"
    Write-Host "Press P to play"
    Write-Host "Press Q to Quit"
}

#Start of Script

#Clear Console
Clear-Host

#Call function
Show-Menu
```

In the code, Clear-Host clears the console of any text; then we call Show-Menu to run the code within it. The great thing about this is we can use the same code anywhere within our scripts simply by calling the function name. Running the code results in the menu displaying to the console as shown in Figure 7-1.

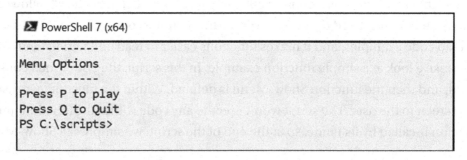

Figure 7-1. *Creating a Show-Menu function*

Passing Parameters

You can also pass values and variables into a function so the function can then work on the information given and possibly return an object as a variable or a collection of objects such as an array.

The values you pass in are called parameters, and they are used to control the behavior of the function you are calling. You can pass as many values as you need and even define the type of parameters that can be accepted, for example, accept integer numbers or strings or both. The function will then take those parameters and use them as required depending on the task the function was built to perform.

Let's do a simple example and create our own adding function, which accepts two [int] variables as its parameters and prints the results out to the console using Write-Host.

```
#Function which adds two int values and returns the results

function Add-Numbers([int]$numberA, [int]$numberB){
    $sumOfNumbers = $numberA + $numberB

    #Display results to console
 Write-Host "Adding 5 and 10 equals: $sumOfNumbers"
}

#Start of Script

#Clear Console
Clear-Host

#Call function
Add-Numbers 5 10
```

If you run this example, you can see the function adding the two number variables and showing the result as shown in Figure 7-2.

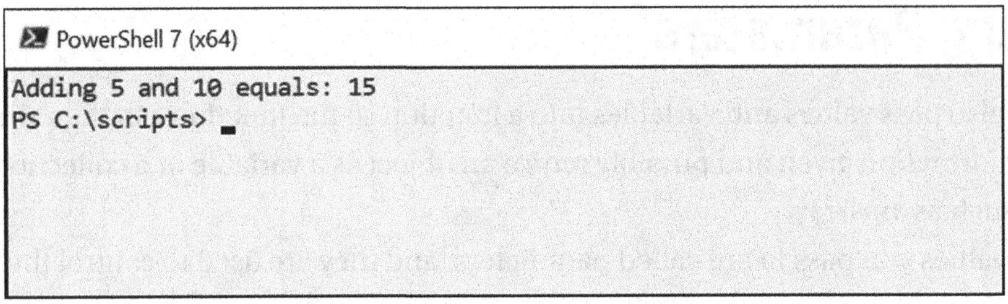

```
PowerShell 7 (x64)

Adding 5 and 10 equals: 15
PS C:\scripts> _
```

Figure 7-2. *Passing variables into a function using parameters*

You can define any number of parameters and variable types you wish to pass into the function. Just add additional parameters by separating them by a , in the brackets after the function name.

```
function Add-Numbers ([int]$numberA, [int]$numberB, [int]$numberC)
```

Returning Objects

Functions can also return a value back to the calling location allowing you to save the returned object for further processing in your script.

Let's extend the previous example and return the result of adding two values.

```
#Function which adds two int values and returns the results

function Add-Numbers([int]$numberA, [int]$numberB){
    $sumOfNumbers = $numberA + $numberB

    #return the value of the results variable
    return $sumOfNumbers
}

#Start of Script

#Clear Console
Clear-Host
```

```
#Call function
$results = Add-Numbers 5 10

#Display results to console
Write-Host "Adding 5 and 10 equals: $results"
```

If you run the code, we get the same output displayed previously in Figure 7-2, only this time the function returns the result back out and into a new variable $results. That variable is then used to write the text out to the console as shown in Figure 7-3.

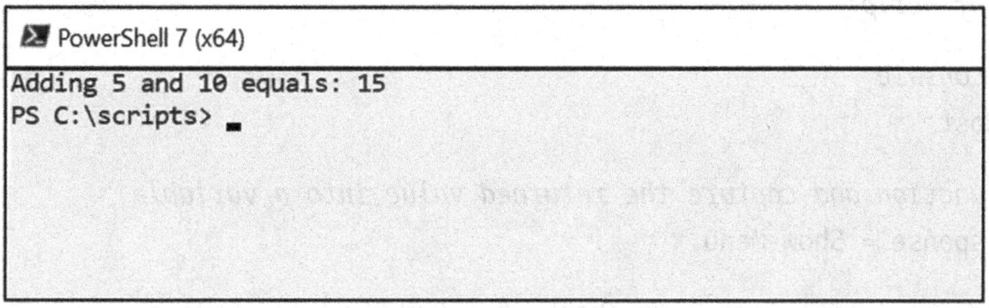

Figure 7-3. *Adding numbers using a function that accepts variables as parameters*

To return an object within your script, simply use the return statement followed by the value or variable. Here the result of passing 5 and 10 into the Add-Numbers function is returned and saved into the $results variable:

```
$results = Add-Numbers 5 10
```

$results can now be used in your script for further processing. Now let's extend our Show-Menu function to capture the user's menu selection and return the result back for further processing. This script captures the user's key press and then compares the response to characters using an if statement.

```
#Beginners Guide to Functions

function Show-Menu{
    #Display menu options
    Write-Host "------------"
    Write-Host "Menu Options"
    Write-Host "------------"
```

```
    Write-Host "Press P to play"
    Write-Host "Press Q to Quit"

    #Capture response from user
    $userResponse = Read-Host -Prompt 'Please select an option'

    #Return the users response variable back out of the function
    return $userResponse
}

#Start of script

#Clear console
Clear-Host

#Call function and capture the returned value into a variable
$userResponse = Show-Menu

#Use and if else statement to check what key the user pressed
if($userResponse -eq 'P'){
    Write-Host "You pressed P to play"
}
elseif($userResponse -eq 'Q'){
    Write-Host "You pressed Q to quit"
}
else{
    Write-Host "You pressed a key not in the menu"
}
```

If we run the code, it displays as per Figure 7-4. The menu text is displayed to the console using the function Show-Menu; it asks the user for a response and returns the value to be used further in the script. In this case, it simply outputs the option selected to the console.

```
PowerShell 7 (x64)
------------
Menu Options
------------
Press P to play
Press Q to Quit
Please select an option: p
You pressed P to play
PS C:\scripts>
```

Figure 7-4. *Using the Show-Menu function and collecting the user's response*

You can see how this script is starting to build out the start screen of your first mini PowerShell game. Awesome work!

Conclusion

Hopefully you are starting to see how easy it is to write scripts using just a few basic commands and statements. Use functions to keep different tasks within your code structured and clean and call them repeatedly as you need them. They are a great way to write code once rather than keep repeating the same blocks over and over.

CHAPTER 8

Classes

A class is another great way to group together code that serves the same purpose, and is used to specify your own objects, which can then be used to save lots of information and passed around as a single object via a variable.

A good example of this is a "Person." A person has multiple properties associated with them. For example, a person has a name, age, height, hair color, favorite colors, and shoe size, to name a few. If you need to create an object that has lots of properties, a class is the best way to group this information together.

In a gaming example, you have players; and players will have position variables, speed, health, a variable to hold their image on the screen, and so on.

Classes also contain function-like groups of code except that in a class they are called methods. Each class you create can have multiple methods, which you can use to group code for common tasks.

In a Player class, you may want to set up a method called Update, which is called to update the player's position and to run code that works out where to move or when to fire a weapon. Let's get stuck in creating a few classes to experiment with.

Classes have some of their own terminology to get used to. For example, a variable defined within a class is called a property. So we will use the word "property" in this chapter a lot, but just remember, all we mean is a variable defined within a class. Classes also have methods, and these are the same as script functions you have seen previously, only they live within a class. We also have class members, and they refer to anything defined within a class, which includes properties. Finally, we have constructors, which are called when an object is created from a class. They are used to set properties to default values and also to have variables passed into the object to have properties set to specified values when created.

Ok, now that you know some of the terminology, let's dive in and create your first class and then explore each part of a class in more depth.

© Ian Waters 2021
I. Waters, *PowerShell for Beginners*, https://doi.org/10.1007/978-1-4842-7064-6_8

Creating Your First Class

Classes can be created at the top of your script or stored in their own files. Some classes can grow quite large, so we will look at how to separate them into their own files later on in the chapter; but for these small examples, we will define them within the same script.

```
Class Person {
    [string]$name

    Person() {
    }
}

$friend = New-Object Person
$friend.name = "Ian"

Write-Host "Hi" $friend.name "how are you?"
```

If you run the code, you will see the output in Figure 8-1. The Person object was created; then we set the variable name and accessed it again to write a message to the console.

PowerShell 7 (x64)
```
PS C:\scripts> .\script.ps1
Hi Ian how are you?
PS C:\scripts> ▄
```

Figure 8-1. *Creating your first class*

In the preceding example, the class is defined by the Class statement followed by a name. It's good practice to call a class by the thing it represents and also start the name with a capital letter making it easier to distinguish it from a variable.

All of the class code is stored within the { } brackets, and variables are defined first. In the preceding example, we define a class called Person with a variable $name.

To create a new object from the class, we need to use the New-Object cmdlet and save the object into a variable, in our case $friend:

```
$friend = New-Object Person
```

To access a property within the class, use a . followed by the property name. You can use this to get or set the value of variables:

```
$friend.name = "Ian"
Write-Host "Hi" $friend.name "how are you?"
```

Properties

Variables used within a class are called properties, and we access them using a special automatic variable called $this, which refers to the current class. You can't access the properties of a class internally or in the usual way as it results in an error when trying to run the code.

For example, trying to set the $name property as in the following

```
$name = "Rebecca"
```

results in the following error:

```
ParserError: C:\scripts\script.ps1:15:9
Line |
  15 |             $name = "Rebecca"
     |             ~~~~~
     | Cannot assign property, use '$this.name'.
```

Setting it via the automatic variable $this works just fine:

```
$this.name = "Rebecca"
```

Having to set parameters via $this can cause some confusion when passing values around because it means you can't differentiate internal properties from parameters being passed into constructors and methods as we will see in the next section.

Constructors

Constructors are used when creating a class object. You can use them to pass in different parameters to set up the class properties. In our Person class example, the constructor takes the name of the class:

```
Person() {
}
```

This constructor is called by default because we didn't pass any parameters into it and this was the only match, so it was called during the creation process.

Let's create a second constructor, into which we can pass the person's name.

```
Class Person {
    [string]$name

    Person() {
    }

    Person([string]$name){
        $this.name = $name
    }
}
$friend = New-Object Person "Rebecca"
$friend.name
```

You can add as many constructors as you need, each accepting different parameters. This gives your class more flexibility when it's used within your code.

Methods

Methods are like functions and allow you to group logical code together in a repeatable block. Methods can be passed objects, and they can also return them if you choose. In our game example, the Player class is great for storing values relating to each player in the game, but we also want each player to perform actions within the game. You can use methods to update the position of the player or to decide what action to take next.

When defining methods in your classes, it's recommended to use a different naming convention compared to when writing a function within your script. Your function will look like Get-Name, but for a method, it's best to use GetName. This makes it easier to see the difference between functions and methods more easily when reading the code.

In the next example, let's create a Player class with a few basic variables to keep track of the name, position, health, and speed; but also let's create a method that displays the values of these variables. Calling this DisplayPlayerStats method at any point within the script will allow us to easily see the values. This can be useful for debugging problems with code at a later date and demonstrates how to set up a very simple method and how to call it.

```
Class Player{

    #Define variables
    [string]$name
    [int]$positionX
    [int]$positionY
    [int]$health
    [int]$speed

    #Class contructor
    Player(){
    }

    #Define methods
    DisplayPlayerStats(){
        Write-Host "Name:" $this.name
        Write-Host "Position X:" $this.positionX
        Write-Host "Position Y:" $this.positionY
        Write-Host "Health:" $this.health
        Write-Host "Speed:" $this.speed
    }
}
```

```
#Create player object
$gamePlayer = New-Object Player

#Set player variables
$gamePlayer.name = "Vincent"
$gamePlayer.positionX = 10
$gamePlayer.positionY = 10
$gamePlayer.health = 100
$gamePlayer.speed = 5

#Dump players stats (useful for debugging problems)
$gamePlayer.DisplayPlayerStats()
```

If you run the script the output will look like Figure 8-2 displaying the value of the variables stored within the object.

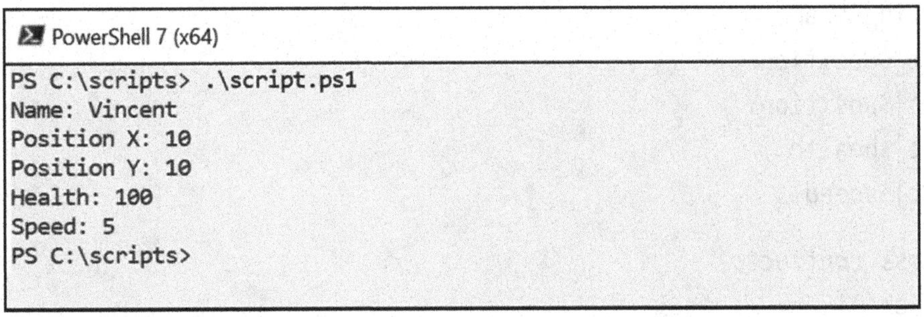

Figure 8-2. *Using class methods*

Passing Parameters

Passing parameters into a method is done in the same way you would with a function. Simply set up a method and define the variable types and names within the () brackets. Then when you call the method, pass in the variables. The only difference when passing variables into a method is that you enter them within () brackets.

```
Class Player {
    #Define variables
    [string]$name
    [int]$positionX
    [int]$positionY
    [int]$health
```

```powershell
    [int]$speed

    #Class contructor
    Player() {
    }

    #Define methods
    DisplayPlayerStats() {
        Write-Host "Name:" $this.name
        Write-Host "Position X:" $this.positionX
        Write-Host "Position Y:" $this.positionY
        Write-Host "Health:" $this.health
        Write-Host "Speed:" $this.speed
    }

    SetPosition([int]$x, [int]$y) {
        $this.positionX = $x
        $this.positionY = $y
    }
}

#Create player object
$gamePlayer = New-Object Player

#Set player variables
$gamePlayer.name = "Vincent"
$gamePlayer.positionX = 10
$gamePlayer.positionY = 10
$gamePlayer.health = 100
$gamePlayer.speed = 5

#Move player to position 20 20
$gamePlayer.SetPosition(20, 20)

#Dump players stats (useful for debugging problems)
$gamePlayer.DisplayPlayerStats()
```

Running the code, we can see that calling the DisplayPlayerStats method writes out all of the parameter values to the console as shown in Figure 8-3.

```
PowerShell 7 (x64)
PS C:\scripts> .\script.ps1
Name: Vincent
Position X: 20
Position Y: 20
Health: 100
Speed: 5
PS C:\scripts>
```

Figure 8-3. Passing values into methods as parameters

In the preceding example, we used a method to set the position of the player. Why would we want to use a method instead of just setting the properties directly? Well, it depends on whether you need a few things to happen when you set property values or not. Maybe you have some properties that can't be set directly because they depend on values of other properties that will need to be set first. It's always good practice to set and get property values via methods where you can, but it's not essential.

Returning Objects

To return objects from a method, simply use the return keyword followed by the value or variable. Once return is called, code execution will stop within the method and the object returned to the caller immediately.

Let's create a method called IsDead, which returns a true or false value when called depending on whether the health variable is less than or equal to zero:

```
[bool]IsDead()
{
    if ($this.health -le 0) {
        return $true
    }
    else {
        return $false
    }
}
```

Notice here that unlike a function, we can define the return object type by adding it to the start of the method. In this case, we are returning a $true or $false value, which is a bool object type, so we add [bool] before the method name that sets the expected return type. If you were returning a string, you would add [string] just like when you define variable and property types.

Doing this makes reading the code easier and explicitly defines what type of value you want to return.

Once called, you can save the returned value to a variable and use it within your script.

```
#Check if the player is dead or alive
$isDead = $gamePlayer.IsDead()
```

Conclusion

Classes are a way to create your own objects, which can be passed around your scripts with ease. This is a great way to store lots of values and define common tasks in a separate code file. In a game, using one class that can represent players and other items cuts down on the amount of code you would need to write. This type of coding practice is called object-oriented programming.

CHAPTER 9

Customizing the Console

The PowerShell console can be customized to suit your needs. You can set the window's title text, which appears in the top-left corner, set the size of the window, and even change the background and text colors.

To get access to the window properties, we call the Get-Host cmdlet and then access the window via ui.rawui. Once we have access to the window, we can start customizing it!

```
$psHost = Get-Host
$window = $psHost.ui.rawui
```

Customizing the Title and Text Colors

Within the window object, you can simply set the .WindowTitle, .ForegroundColour, and .BackgroundColor properties directly to change the look of your console window.

In the following script, setting the text to red and the background to black gives it a real dark feel, perfect for a battle with a dragon in an adventure game, maybe?

```
#Get the console window
$psHost = Get-Host
$window = $psHost.ui.rawui

#Set the window properties
$window.WindowTitle = "My PowerShell Game"
$window.ForegroundColor = "Red"
$window.BackgroundColor = "Black"
```

© Ian Waters 2021
I. Waters, *PowerShell for Beginners*, https://doi.org/10.1007/978-1-4842-7064-6_9

```
#Clear the console
Clear-Host

Write-Host "Wow this is fun!"
```

Running this code turns all the text to the set foreground color. Notice that it even changes the color of the console prompt, not just the text you output to it from the script, as shown in Figure 9-1.

Figure 9-1. *Changing the console title text and background and text colors*

You will learn more about colors in Chapter 11, but here is a reference of the available built-in color definitions you can use to change the background and font colors:

"Black"
"Blue"
"Cyan"
"DarkBlue"
"DarkCyan"
"DarkGray"
"DarkGreen"
"DarkMagenta"
"DarkRed"
"DarkYellow"
"Gray"
"Green"
"Magenta"
"Red"
"White"
"Yellow"

As you can see in Figure 9-2, this is getting interesting. Look at all the colors you can start introducing into your scripts!

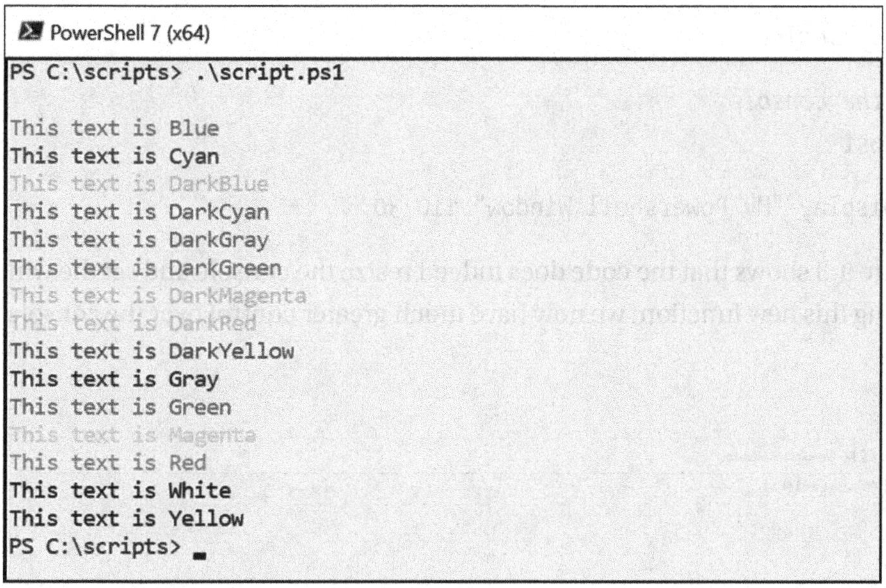

```
PowerShell 7 (x64)
PS C:\scripts> .\script.ps1

This text is Blue
This text is Cyan
This text is DarkBlue
This text is DarkCyan
This text is DarkGray
This text is DarkGreen
This text is DarkMagenta
This text is DarkRed
This text is DarkYellow
This text is Gray
This text is Green
This text is Magenta
This text is Red
This text is White
This text is Yellow
PS C:\scripts> _
```

Figure 9-2. *Changing the color of specific text*

Resizing the Console

To get a nice-sized gaming screen or to make room for a large menu screen, you will need to set the number of text lines (height) and the number of characters per line (width). For ease of use, in the following, I created a function that can be called to set the title, width, and height. It can be called at any time throughout your scripts to change the window as required.

```
function Setup-Display([string]$title, [int]$width, [int]$height) {
    $psHost = get-host
    $window = $psHost.ui.rawui
    $newsize = $window.WindowSize
    $newsize.Height = $height
    $newsize.Width = $width
```

```
    $window.WindowSize = $newsize
    $window.WindowTitle = $title
}

#Start of script

#Clear the console
Clear-Host

Setup-Display "My Powershell Window" 110 30
```

Figure 9-3 shows that the code does indeed resize the console and set the window title. Using this new function, we now have much greater control over the console window.

Figure 9-3. *Using the Setup-Display cmdlet to change the look of the Powershell console*

Conclusion

Gaining control of the PowerShell console window opens up some great customization possibilities. From here, we have set up our gaming window. Now let the fun commence!

## CHAPTER 10

User Input

In this chapter, we are going to learn how to read input from the user in the form of key presses and strings of text. If you present a menu to the user, you need a way to see which option they pressed or what words they have typed. Once you have learned how to read key presses and text from the keyboard, we can build on it to produce a small text-based adventure game in the next chapter! We will look at other types of user input later on in Chapter 17 when we look at reading files, which is another form of user input. For now, we are going to read key presses and strings of text and numbers.

Reading a Key Press

Ok, let's crack on and start interacting with the user by reading key presses. You have briefly seen how to do this in a previous chapter, but let's take a close look at a few more methods to read user input.

Let's start off by writing a function to read a single character typed in; let's call it Read-Character.

Within the function, we access the PowerShell console via $host.ui.RawUI. From here, we can see if the KeyAvailable property is equal to $true or $false. If there's a KeyAvailable, then read it using the method ReadKey.

Whenever a user types into the console, the characters are queued up in an input buffer. This means that if you read a key, it won't necessarily be the last key the user typed or intended to enter as a response to a question from the script. To avoid issues with this, you can use $host.ui.RawUI.FlushInputBuffer() at the start of your script to clear out any logged key presses. Then the next time you call our Read-Character function, it should return the last character the user typed.

© Ian Waters 2021
I. Waters, *PowerShell for Beginners*, https://doi.org/10.1007/978-1-4842-7064-6_10

Let's start by writing a function to check if a key press is available and return the character if there is one and a $null if not:

```
function Read-Character() {
    if ($host.ui.RawUI.KeyAvailable) {
        return $Host.UI.RawUI.ReadKey("NoEcho,IncludeKeyDown").Character
    }

    return $null
}
```

In this function, we first use an if statement to see if there is a key press waiting to be read. If there is, it returns the Character variable by calling the ReadKey method. If there is no key available, then the default action of the function is to return a $null value.

Now let's use this function in a small demo script, which reads a character from the user and then displays it to the screen. When the user presses the "Q" key, the script exists.

```
#Variables
$done = $false

function Read-Character() {
    if ($host.ui.RawUI.KeyAvailable) {
        return $Host.UI.RawUI.ReadKey("NoEcho,IncludeKeyDown").Character
    }

    return $null
}

#Clear console
Clear-Host

#Clear any pre existing key presses
$host.ui.RawUI.FlushInputBuffer()

Write-Host "Press any key or q to quit"

#Keep looping round checking for new key presses
#Loop round while done is not (!) equal to true
while (!$done) {
    #Check for new key presses
    $char = Read-Character
```

```
if ($char -ne $null) {
    Write-Host "You pressed $char"

    #If the key press equals q then exit the loop
    if ($char -eq 'q') {
        $done = $true
    }
}
}
}
```

You can see from the script that we use a variable $done, which is first set to $false. This allows the script to enter a while loop, which calls our Read-Character function. The returned character is then checked to see if it equals a $null value. If it does, the loop continues and checks for a pressed character. If the returned character is not equal to $null, then it displays the pressed key to the console.

Finally, it also checks if the pressed key equals "Q" and if it does sets the $done variable to $true, which then exits the while loop, and the script completes.

If we run the script, you can see it waits for a key press and writes it out to the console; and if we press Q, the script exits as shown in Figure 10-1.

```
 My Powershell Window
Press any key or q to quit
You pressed A
You pressed D
You pressed F
You pressed E
You pressed W
You pressed Q
PS C:\scripts>
```

Figure 10-1. *Reading key presses*

Read a Line of Text

If you want to read a full line of text up to the user pressing Enter, you can use the built-in cmdlet Read-Host. This will wait for the user to type in some text and press Enter and will return a string back to your script, which you can then store into a variable. Read-Host has a neat parameter -Prompt, which allows you to ask a question and then read in the line of text.

In the following example, we clear the screen and then ask "What is your name?" The cmdlet then waits for the user to type their name and press Enter. We grab the answer into the variable $userResponse and write them a nice message back.

```
#Clear console
Clear-Host

#Ask questions using -Prompt
$userResponse = Read-Host -Prompt 'What is your name? '
Write-Host "Hi $userResponse nice to meet you!"

#Read input from next line
Write-Host "Where are you from?"
$userResponse = Read-Host
```

If you run this code example it will prompt you to answer the questions. The text you type is saved into a variable and used to customise the output to the console as shown in Figure 10-2.

```
 My Powershell Window
What is your name? : Ian
Hi Ian nice to meet you!
Where are you from?
Bexhill
PS C:\scripts> ▄
```

Figure 10-2. *Reading a line of text typed into the PowerShell console*

Conclusion

Reading input from the user during gameplay is vital and can be needed when writing more generalized scripts to allow the user to set parameters or to select options from a menu. Combine user input with conditional statements if and else, while loops, switch statements, and then calling functions and cmdlets, and you can see how easy it is to set up a basic menu system for scripts and games of your own design.

## CHAPTER 11

Dragon Slayer

This is where I start to geek out and get all nostalgic for really old-school 1980s computers and games. This is a version of a script I wrote a few years ago when I started playing with PowerShell. It really got me into it and was one of the reasons I wanted to write this book. If it got me more pumped about learning and writing PowerShell, hopefully it will do the same for you.

This chapter is going to combine a little of everything we have learned so far into a playable old-school-style text adventure game I call Dragon Slayer!

Code Design

Let's first start by defining what the game will do, and that will give us a clearer idea of the functions we will need to write and how the main game loop will work:

- Set up the console window.

- Title screen.

- Character selection screen.

- Accept the quest.

- Story sections.

- Quit the game.

We've set up the console window before, so we can reuse the Setup-Display function we have already.

The title screen will display and wait for a key press. Then the script will enter the main game loop where the player chooses a character, accepts the quest, and then enters the main story sections.

© Ian Waters 2021
I. Waters, *PowerShell for Beginners*, https://doi.org/10.1007/978-1-4842-7064-6_11

The character selection, acceptance of the quest, and story sections will be divided up into their own functions. So to move the player through the game, we just have to call the function for the current place in the player's experience.

To display the title screen, we can simply call a function like Title-Screen. The Title-Screen function can then display the title screen graphics and wait for the player to press a key.

Once the Title-Screen function returns, we can then call the next function, Character-Selection. Again this function will display some text or graphics and wait for the player to choose a character by entering 1, 2, 3, or 4 and pressing the Enter key. The function will then set a global variable to save the player's selection so we can use it later on in the game.

Next, we can all a function called Accept-TheQuest, and its job will be to set the scene of the story line. The player can then choose to play the game or exit the game completely.

If the player decides to play, we can simply call the first story section, which will again be its own function. First, we need to define the story and what choices the player can make in each section.

Sometimes when coding larger and more complex scripts, I break out a pen and paper and think about how I can divide the tasks up. This helps to figure out what functions or classes I need and makes building out the script easier. Always spend some time designing your scripts first as it will make the whole process easier. Since I'm writing this book, let's use the power of a flowchart instead!

See in Figure 11-1 I have laid out the flow of the script. Using this, I started to see what functions I needed to implement. Do this when writing your own scripts as it will help massively.

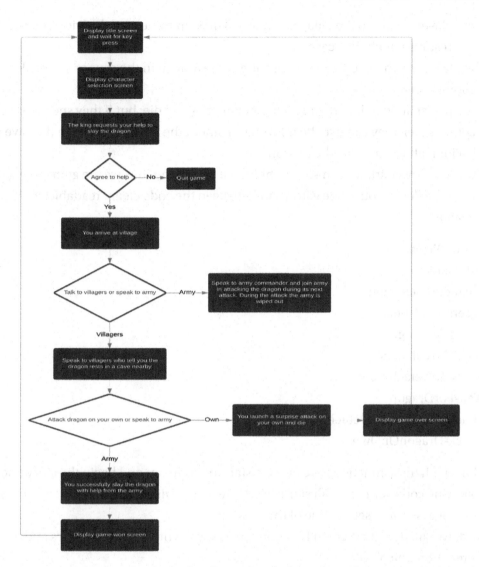

Figure 11-1. *Diagram showing the flow of code based on decisions made in the game*

Defining the Functions

The flowchart gives us a clear idea of how the story will flow, and basically the player accepts the quest and goes to the village being attacked. The player can choose to speak to the villagers or speak to the commander in charge of a small force assigned to deal with the problem.

If the player speaks to the villagers, they will pick up some useful advice that the dragon is resting at night in a cave nearby.

The player can then decide to go and attack the dragon in the cave or go speak to the army commander.

If the player attacks the dragon on their own, they will die; but if they speak to the army commander, they can use the information about the dragon resting in the cave to launch a joint attack and slay the dragon.

Using the flowchart, we can start to build out a few functions we are going to need to manage the flow through the game and help keep the code clean, readable, and manageable:

Setup-Display
Title-Screen
Character-Selection
Accept-TheQuest
Arrive-AtVillage
Speak-ToVillagers
Speak-ToDetachment
Wait-ForDragon
Attack-DragonWithDetachment
Attack-DragonOnOwn

Along with these functions, we need to start the script up and begin the story line. The following code is where it all starts. First, the Setup-Display function is called to set up the display size and set the title of the window.

Next, we call the Title-Screen function to display the title screen graphics and wait for a key press from the player.

Next, we need a while loop to keep the game active while the global variable runGame is equal to $true. When the player decides to not help the king deal with the dragon, the runGame variable is set to $false, and the main game loop exits and the script finishes.

Once the main game loop is running, the Character-Selection function is called, which displays the list of available characters and saves the player's choice into a global variable.

Next, the Accept-TheQuest function is called, and the player can choose to help the king or quit the game. The result is returned as a Boolean value from the function. We capture the returned value into a variable and use an if statement to either continue playing the game by calling Arrive-AtVillage or quit the game and set the global variable runGame to $false, which will exit the game loop, and the script will exit.

Take a look at the following code, which starts to flesh out this flow. We set up the console using Setup-Display and then enter the title screen. From there, we enter the main script loop where we wait for the user to select a character and accept the quest. If they accept the quest, we start the main flow for the story.

```
Setup-Display "Dragon Slayer" 64 38

Title-Screen

while ($global:runGame) {

    Character-Selection

    $accept = Accept-TheQuest

    if ($accept -eq $true) {
        Arrive-AtVillage
    }
    else {
        #Player Quit
        Write-Host ""
        Write-Host "Thanks for Playing"
        $global:runGame = $false
        Start-Sleep 3
    }
}
```

If the player accepts the quest, the Arrive-AtVillage function is called, which starts the game's flow. From this function, the player makes a choice, which then calls the appropriate function for the choice made.

Creating the Title Screen

Let's take a look at how you can build out a simple title screen with ASCII (American Standard Code for Information Interchange) graphics generated from an online generator.

Here I'm using the Write-Host cmdlet and manually copying in each line from the generated ASCII file. At the bottom of the function, I call Read-NextKey and save the response into the variable $continue. I then use an if statement to determine the next course of action. In this case, the player can press Q to quit the game. The global variable runGame is then set to false so that the main game loop doesn't start and the script exists. If the player presses any other key, then the script enters the main game loop.

All other functions in this simple example follow the same format. On-screen graphics are displayed, and a response is captured from the player. An if else statement is then used to determine which function to call next to progress the story line.

To fit the code onto the pages of this book, I've written a smaller version of the original here. You can find this version and the original more impressive-looking version in the code files for this book.

```
function Title-Screen() {
    #Clear any pre existing key presses
    $host.ui.RawUI.FlushInputBuffer()

    Clear-Host

    Write-Host "                                                               "
    Write-Host " @@@@`                                      @@@@ @@             "
    Write-Host " @@ @@                                      @,   @@             "
    Write-Host " @@ :@',@@@ @@@@@ @@@@  @@  @@@@  @@@` @@ @@@@.@@ @@: @@@ ,@@@   "
    Write-Host " @@ `@@ @@@   '@@ @  @ @ @@ @'@@   @@@ @@    @ @@ @@ @ @@:@@@     "
    Write-Host " @@ #@, @   @:@@@ @  @ @ +@ @ :@  ;;@@ @@ @@:@ @@ @@,@@@@@ @      "
    Write-Host " @@@@@ ,@# ;@ '@@ @@#@ @: @ @@:@@ @'@@ @@ @@ @` @@@@ @  :,:@      "
    Write-Host " @@@'  ,@# @@+@@ :,@@; @@  @@:@@ @@@@ @@ @@@@`  @@: +@@@ ,@       "
    Write-Host "                 :; @@                        @@                "
    Write-Host "                  @@@@,                      @@'               "
    Write-Host "                                                               "
    Write-Host "                              @                                "
```

```powershell
    Write-Host "                            ,#++,  @                                          "
    Write-Host "                            ,;+@@@@                                        .;"
    Write-Host "                          #'.'@@@@@@#                          :@@@@@"
    Write-Host "           '              @@@@@+@+@@             :            ,@@@@@@@@@"
    Write-Host "  @@@;          @       ,..@@@`@@@@@@+         @         +@@@@@@@@@@@"
    Write-Host "  :'@@@;       @      +@@@@;@@:`@@@         @       +@@@;:  :@@@@ "
    Write-Host "  @@@@@@@.    @,      .::@@@.:@@@ `:        @;    ;@@@@@@@@@@`;` "
    Write-Host "  @@@@@@@@@@@@      @@@@:`  @;  `         ,@@@@@@@@@@@@@@@@   "
    Write-Host "  @@@@@@@@@@@@      :,@@@@@   @#@            @@@@@@@@@@@@@@@   "
    Write-Host "  @@@@@@;@@@@@      # @@@@@ ::            @@@@@:@@@@@@@   "
    Write-Host "  @@@@@.@@@@@@@@@        @@@@@             `@@@@@@@#+@@@@@:   "
    Write-Host "  @@@@ @@@@@@@@@@@@`       @@@@@          :@@@@@@@@@@@@ @@@@   "
    Write-Host "  ,#@@@@@@@@@@@@@@ @@@@@@@@@@@@@@@@@@@@@@:@@@@@@@@@@@@.+   "
    Write-Host "       `@@@@@ @@@@@@@@@@@@@@@@@@@@@@,@@@@@                   "
    Write-Host "          @@@@,@@@@@@@@@@@@@@@@@@@@@@ @@@+                   "
    Write-Host "         @@+@@@@@@@@@@@@@@@@@@@@@@@;@@+                   "
    Write-Host "         @:@@@@@@@@@@@@@@@@@@@@@@@@@@@                   "
    Write-Host "         ,`@@.   @@@@@@@@@@@@@   .@@;                   "
    Write-Host "        .       @@@@@@@@@@@@@       ',                   "
    Write-Host "                       #@@@@@@@`                         "
    Write-Host "                       :@@@@@                           "
    Write-Host "                       ;@@@@                           "
    Write-Host "                                                        "
    Write-Host "            Press Any Key to Play or Q to quit          "

    $continue = Read-NextKey

    if ($continue -eq 'q') {
        $global:runGame = $false
    }
}

Clear-Host
Title-Screen
```

Script Variables

In the game, I use three variables and set them as global so they can be accessed from anywhere in the script. These are used to save the player's chosen character, to check if the game should still be running or if the player quits, and finally to record if the player picked up a special tip from the villagers if the player chose to speak to them:

```
#Game Variables
$global:playerCharacter = $null
$global:playerDragonTip = $false
$global:runGame = $true
```

Let's Put It All Together

Now that we know how the script will flow and what functions we need, we can start to assemble everything together. Each of the functions will follow the same setup. They will first clear the console using Clear-Host and then use Write-Host to write text out to the screen. Then they will read a key press on the keyboard and either return a value or call the next function in the flow. Once the player enters the story line, each function will call the next as they progress through the story until they are killed or complete their quest!

Spend time reviewing this code and try to follow along and play the game just by looking at the code. I will help you understand how it works and will show the use of various coding skills you have learned from previous chapters in the book.

```
#Game Variables
$global:playerCharacter = $null
$global:playerDragonTip = $false
$global:runGame = $true

function Setup-Display([string]$title, [int]$width, [int]$height) {
    $psHost = Get-Host
    $window = $psHost.ui.rawui
    $newsize = $window.WindowSize
    $newsize.Height = $height
    $newsize.Width = $width
```

```powershell
    $window.WindowSize = $newsize
    $window.WindowTitle = $title
}

function Read-NextKey() {
    return $Host.UI.RawUI.ReadKey("NoEcho,IncludeKeyDown").Character
}

function Title-Screen() {
    #Clear any pre existing key presses
    $host.ui.RawUI.FlushInputBuffer()

    Clear-Host

    Write-Host "                                                                    "
    Write-Host " @@@@`                                         @@@@ @@               "
    Write-Host " @@ @@                                        @,   @@               "
    Write-Host " @@ :@',@@@ @@@@@ @@@@  @@  @@@@  @@@` @@ @@@@.@@ @@: @@@ ,@@@ "
    Write-Host " @@ `@@ @@@    '@@ @  @ @ @@ @'@@     @@@ @@   @ @@ @@ @  @@:@@@ "
    Write-Host " @@ #@, @   @:@@@ @  @ @ +@ @ :@   ;;@@ @@ @@:@ @@ @@,@@@@@ @   "
    Write-Host " @@@@@ ,@# ;@ '@@ @@#@ @@: @ @@:@@ @'@@ @@ @@ @` @@@@ @  :,:@   "
    Write-Host " @@@'   ,@#  @@+@@ :,@@; @@  @@:@@ @@@@ @@ @@@@`  @@: +@@@ ,@   "
    Write-Host "                :; @@                         @@               "
    Write-Host "                  @@@@,                      @@'              "
    Write-Host "                                                               "
    Write-Host "                         @                                     "
    Write-Host "                       ,#++, @                                 "
    Write-Host "                        ,;+@@@@                             .;"
    Write-Host "                      #'.'@@@@@@#                      :@@@@@"
    Write-Host "              '        @@@@@+@+@@           :       ,@@@@@@@@"
    Write-Host " @@@;         @      ,..@@@`@@@@@@+       @        +@@@@@@@@@@"
    Write-Host " :'@@@;        @      +@@@@;@@:`@@@        @      +@@@;:: :@@@@ "
    Write-Host " @@@@@@@.    @,       .::@@@.:@@@ `:       @;  ;@@@@@@@@@@`;` "
    Write-Host " @@@@@@@@@@@@         @@@@:`  @;  `        ,@@@@@@@@@@@@@@@@ "
    Write-Host " @@@@@@@@@@@@         :,@@@@@  @#@         @@@@@@@@@@@@@@    "
    Write-Host " @@@@@@@;@@@@@        # @@@@@@ ::.         @@@@@:@@@@@@@@    "
    Write-Host " @@@@@.@@@@@@@@@         @@@@@@         `@@@@@@@@#+@@@@@:    "
```

```
Write-Host " @@@@ @@@@@@@@@@@`        @@@@@        :@@@@@@@@@@@ @@@@     "
Write-Host " ,#@@@@@@@@@@@@ @@@@@@@@@@@@@@@@@@@@@@@:@@@@@@@@@@@@.+        "
Write-Host "        `@@@@@ @@@@@@@@@@@@@@@@@@@@@@@@@,@@@@@                "
Write-Host "          @@@@,@@@@@@@@@@@@@@@@@@@@@@@@@@ @@@+               "
Write-Host "          @@+@@@@@@@@@@@@@@@@@@@@@@@@@@;@@+                  "
Write-Host "          @:@@@@@@@@@@@@@@@@@@@@@@@@@@@@@                     "
Write-Host "          ,`@@.   @@@@@@@@@@@@@@   .@@;                       "
Write-Host "          .       @@@@@@@@@@@@@      ',                      "
Write-Host "                    #@@@@@@@`                                "
Write-Host "                     :@@@@@                                  "
Write-Host "                     ;@@@@                                   "
Write-Host "                                                             "
Write-Host "             Press Any Key to Play or Q to quit              "

    $continue = Read-NextKey

    if ($continue -eq 'q') {
        $global:runGame = $false
    }
}

function Character-Selection() {
    #Clear Console
    Clear-Host

    #Dragon Slayer
    Write-Host "###############################################################"
    Write-Host "#                                                             #"
    Write-Host "#            Dragon Slayer 1.0 by Ian Waters                  #"
    Write-Host "#            www.slashadmin.co.uk \ Life In IT                #"
    Write-Host "#            Supporting Awesome IT administrators             #"
    Write-Host "#                                                             #"
    Write-Host "###############################################################"
    Write-Host "                                                             "
    Write-Host "###############################################################"
    Write-Host "                                                             "
    Write-Host "                     Character Selection                     "
```

```
Write-Host "                                                              "
Write-Host "                         A: Slorvak                           "
Write-Host "                         B: Prince Valant                     "
Write-Host "                         C: Zanthe                            "
Write-Host "                         D: Amara                             "
Write-Host "                                                              "
Write-Host "                                                              "
Write-Host "##############################################################"
Write-Host "                                                              "

$userResponse = Read-Host -Prompt "Choose your character"

Write-Host ""

Switch ($userResponse) {
    A { $global:playerCharacter = "Slorvak" }
    B { $global:playerCharacter = "Prince Valant" }
    C { $global:playerCharacter = "Zanthe" }
    D { $global:playerCharacter = "Amara" }
    default { $global:playerCharacter = "Slorvak" }
}

Write-Host "You selected $global:playerCharacter, lets begin"

Start-Sleep 3
}

function Accept-TheQuest() {
    #Clear Console
    Clear-Host

    #Dragon Slayer
    Write-Host "##############################################################"
    Write-Host "#                                                           #"
    Write-Host "# The King requests your help to slay the dragon FireWing.  #"
    Write-Host "# FireWing has been woken from a deep slumber and has started #"
    Write-Host "# terrorising the local villages.                           #"
    Write-Host "#                                                           #"
    Write-Host "# The people are scared and have started to leave the kingdom. #"
```

```
Write-Host "#                                                          #"
Write-Host "# The King must protect his people.                        #"
Write-Host "#                                                          #"
Write-Host "##########################################################"
Write-Host "                                                           "

do {
    $userResponse = Read-Host -Prompt "Are you willing to help?
    (yes/no) "
}
while ($userResponse -notlike "Yes" -and $UserResponse -notlike "No")

Write-Host ""

Switch ($userResponse) {
    "Yes" {
        Write-Host "The King thanks you $global:playerCharacter"
        Write-Host ""
        Write-Host "Now start your quest!"
        Start-Sleep 4
        return $true
    }
    "No" {
        Write-Host "Your King is dissapointed and sends you on your way"
        Start-Sleep 4
        return $false
    }
}
}

function Arrive-AtVillage() {
    Clear-Host

    Write-Host ""
    Write-Host "After two day's ride you arrive at Florin, a small village
    on the"
    Write-Host "outskirts of the kingdom."
    Write-Host ""
```

```
Write-Host "You choose Florin to make your stand due to its remote
location"
Write-Host "and nearby army detachment camping nearby."
Write-Host ""
Write-Host "On your arrival do you?"
Write-Host ""
Write-Host "A) Talk to the villagers"
Write-Host "B) Talk to the commander in charge of the local detachment"
Write-Host ""

do {
    $userResponse = Read-Host -Prompt "Answer (A or B)"
}
while ($userResponse -notlike "A" -and $UserResponse -notlike "B")

Write-Host ""

Switch ($userResponse) {
    "A" { Speak-ToVillagers }
    "B" { Speak-ToDetachment }
}
}

function Speak-ToDetachment() {
    Clear-Host

    if (!$global:playerDragonTip) {
        Write-Host ""
        Write-Host "You speak to Cedric who is commanding the local "
        Write-Host "detachmenSpeat of soldiers."
        Write-Host ""
        Write-Host "Cendric is making his way north to rejoin the rest
        of the"
        Write-Host "troops but is willing toassist in finding FireWing and "
        Write-Host "suggests waiting until the dragon returns and slay it
        in combat."
        Write-Host ""
        Write-Host "Press any key to continue."
```

```
        $continue = Read-NextKey

        Wait-ForDragon
    }
    else {
        Write-Host ""
        Write-Host "You speak to Cedric who is commanding the local
        detachment"
        Write-Host "of soldiers."
        Write-Host ""
        Write-Host "Cendric is making his way north to rejoin the rest of the"
        Write-Host "troops but is willing toassist in finding FireWing."
        Write-Host ""
        Write-Host "You tell Cendric that the local villiagers know where the"
        Write-Host "dragon may be resting at night together you formulate"
        Write-Host "a plan of attack."
        Write-Host ""
        Write-Host "Press any key to continue."

        $continue = Read-NextKey

        Attack-DragonWithDetachment
    }
}

function Wait-ForDragon() {
    Clear-Host

    Write-Host "You setup camp with the detachment and prepare the weapons."
    Write-Host ""
    Write-Host "During the night FireWing attacks the camp and villagers."
    Write-Host "Everyone runs for their life but you are engolfed in flames"
    Write-Host "and dont make it out alive!"
    Write-Host ""
    Write-Host "You have failed to protect the villagers."
    Write-Host ""
```

```
    Write-Host "Game Over"
    Write-Host ""
    Write-Host "Press any key to continue"

    $continue = Read-NextKey
}

function Attack-DragonWithDetachment() {
    Clear-Host

    Write-Host "You ready your weapons and with the villiagers help you"
    Write-Host "formulate a plan. The plan is to setup a large chainmail"
    Write-Host "net over the cave entrance."
    Write-Host ""
    Write-Host "When FireWing enters the cave to rest you will drop the"
    Write-Host "net to block his escape."
    Write-Host ""
    Write-Host "The troops will then fire their bows into the cave and"
    Write-Host "slay the dragon!"
    Write-Host ""
    Write-Host "You work with Cedric and the troops to prepare the trap"
    Write-Host "and wait in hiding."
    Write-Host ""
    Write-Host "During the night FireWing enters the cave and the trap"
    Write-Host "is sprung. Huge arrows are fired into the cave and fire"
    Write-Host "bellows out from the cave entrance. More arrows fly and"
    Write-Host "then silence.."
    Write-Host ""
    Write-Host "You enter the cave and and find nothing but a pile of"
    Write-Host "ash on the floor."
    Write-Host ""
    Write-Host "Congratulations! you have defeated FireWing and"
    Write-Host "protected the Kingdom."
    Write-Host ""
    Write-Host "You are indeed a cunning and mighty warrior!"
    Write-Host ""
    Write-Host "Press any key to continue."
```

```
        $Continue = Read-NextKey
}

function Attack-DragonOnOwn() {
    Clear-Host

    Write-Host ""
    Write-Host "After dark Hadrain takes you to the cave and leaves you to"
    Write-Host "investigate."
    Write-Host ""
    Write-Host "You get close to the cave but cant see any sign of FireWing"
    Write-Host "so you move close still."
    Write-Host ""
    Write-Host "Suddenly you hear a noise from behind! you turn quickly"
    Write-Host "and are engolved by flames!"
    Write-Host ""
    Write-Host "FireWing as struck you down with his fire breath and you"
    Write-Host "are turned to ashes."
    Write-Host ""
    Write-Host "Press any key to continue"

        $Continue = Read-NextKey
}

function Speak-ToVillagers() {
    Clear-Host

    Write-Host ""
    Write-Host "You speak to Hadrain an elder of the village who explains that "
    Write-Host "FireWing has been seen resting in a cave nearby after
    nightfall."
    Write-Host "He suggests speaking to the local detachment and launching
    a surprise"
    Write-Host "attack after dark with their help.   "
    Write-Host ""
    Write-Host "What do you do next?"
    Write-Host ""
    Write-Host "A) Speak to the detachments commander"
```

```
Write-Host "B) Ask Hadarin to take you to the cave after dark"
Write-Host ""

#Player has picked up a tip from the local villagers!
#This will change the outcome of future decisions
$global:playerDragonTip = $true

do {
    $UserResponse = Read-Host -Prompt "Answer (A or B)"
}
while ($UserResponse -notlike "A" -and $UserResponse -notlike "B")

Write-Host ""

Switch ($UserResponse) {
    "A" { Speak-ToDetachment }
    "B" { Attack-DragonOnOwn }
}
}

Setup-Display "Dragon Slayer" 64 38

Title-Screen

while ($global:runGame) {
    Character-Selection

    $accept = Accept-TheQuest

    if ($accept -eq $true) {
        Arrive-AtVillage
    }
    else {
        #Player Quit
        Write-Host ""
        Write-Host "Thanks for Playing"
        $global:runGame = $false
        Start-Sleep 3
    }
}
```

See, it's not that complicated when broken down into individual functions. This example demonstrates how useful functions are in keeping your code clean and readable. Each function has a specific job making developing the code further becomes much easier.

In Figures 11-2 and 11-3, there are a few screenshots from the script showing how the game looks when run directly within Windows.

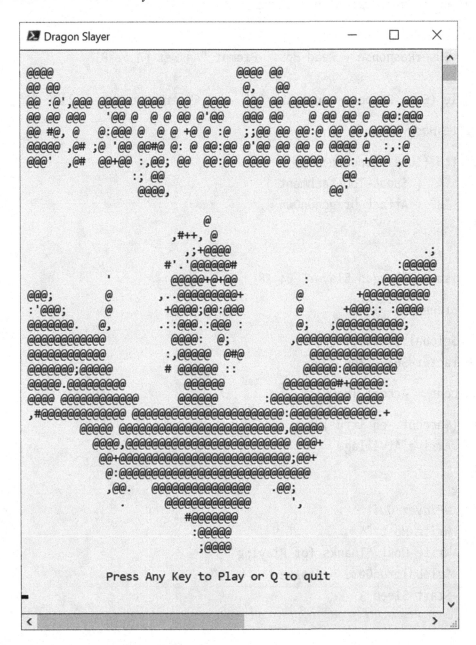

Figure 11-2. *Dragon Slayer title screen*

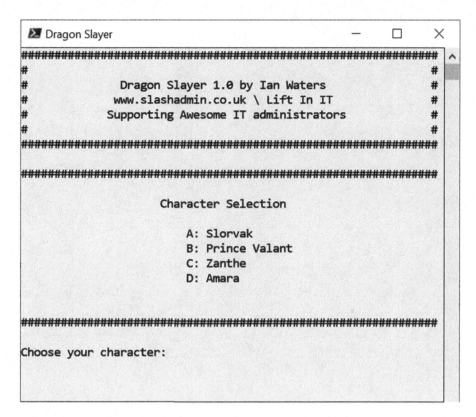

Figure 11-3. Dragon Slayer character selection menu

Conclusion

Dragon Slayer was the first real demonstration of your PowerShell skills, and it still only uses some very basic coding statements: conditional statements if and else, while loops, switch statements, and calling functions and cmdlets. Here you can see how easy it is to set up basic menu systems for scripts and games of your own design.

It would be awesome to see any additions or versions of this game. Send me an email at ian@slashadmin.co.uk with your code as I would love to post it on the site to share.

Now that you can create awesome menu systems, let's see how to add a bit of color to your text!

## CHAPTER 12

Getting Colorful

In this chapter, you are going to learn how to change the color of text written out to the console. We will look at all of the text color options available including background colors and then explore how to customize the background color of the PowerShell console itself. Adding a splash of color to your scripts can help make the text more readable and specific items stand out more. If you need to display an error message, then make it red. If a script has successfully performed a task, then let the user know by using some green text. Let's dive in.

Changing Font Color

Adding some color to your scripts is easy when using the Write-Host cmdlet. It allows you to specify a predefined color by specifying it in the -ForegroundColor parameter. The following is a script that will output each of the available predefined colors in PowerShell. Adding red to error messages and green to indicate success in your scripts is a great way to highlight issues to the end user. In a game, we can use them to make it more interesting and playable.

Run the following script to see how the text will look using each of the predefined colors.

```
Write-Host "This text is Black" -ForegroundColor Black
Write-Host "This text is Blue" -ForegroundColor Blue
Write-Host "This text is Cyan" -ForegroundColor Cyan
Write-Host "This text is DarkBlue" -ForegroundColor DarkBlue
Write-Host "This text is DarkCyan" -ForegroundColor DarkCyan
Write-Host "This text is DarkGray" -ForegroundColor DarkGray
Write-Host "This text is DarkGreen" -ForegroundColor DarkGreen
Write-Host "This text is DarkMagenta" -ForegroundColor DarkMagenta
```

© Ian Waters 2021
I. Waters, *PowerShell for Beginners*, https://doi.org/10.1007/978-1-4842-7064-6_12

```
Write-Host "This text is DarkRed" -ForegroundColor DarkRed
Write-Host "This text is DarkYellow" -ForegroundColor DarkYellow
Write-Host "This text is Gray" -ForegroundColor Gray
Write-Host "This text is Green" -ForegroundColor Green
Write-Host "This text is Magenta" -ForegroundColor Magenta
Write-Host "This text is Red" -ForegroundColor Red
Write-Host "This text is White" -ForegroundColor White
Write-Host "This text is Yellow" -ForegroundColor Yellow
```

If we run the script, as shown in Figure 12-1, you can see all of the colors available. Look how well they stand out and can be used to highlight text output from your script.

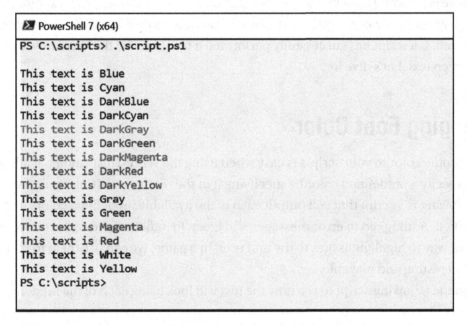

Figure 12-1. *Changing text color when using the Write-Host cmdlet*

Changing Background Color

Changing the background color will change the color behind the text that is output to the console.

Run the following script to see how each line looks when using the specified background colors.

```
Write-Host "This text is displayed using..." -BackgroundColor Black
Write-Host "This text is displayed using..." -BackgroundColor Blue
Write-Host "This text is displayed using..." -BackgroundColor Cyan
Write-Host "This text is displayed using..." -BackgroundColor DarkBlue
Write-Host "This text is displayed using..." -BackgroundColor DarkCyan
Write-Host "This text is displayed using..." -BackgroundColor DarkGray
Write-Host "This text is displayed using..." -BackgroundColor DarkGreen
Write-Host "This text is displayed using..." -BackgroundColor DarkMagenta
Write-Host "This text is displayed using..." -BackgroundColor DarkRed
Write-Host "This text is displayed using..." -BackgroundColor DarkYellow
Write-Host "This text is displayed using..." -BackgroundColor Gray
Write-Host "This text is displayed using..." -BackgroundColor Green
Write-Host "This text is displayed using..." -BackgroundColor Magenta
Write-Host "This text is displayed using..." -BackgroundColor Red
Write-Host "This text is displayed using..." -BackgroundColor White
Write-Host "This text is displayed using..." -BackgroundColor Yellow
```

Figure 12-2 Shows the output of the script to the console. Background colours are a great way to highlight error messages or warnings to the user.

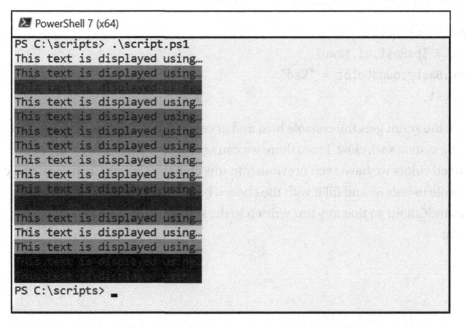

Figure 12-2. *Changing text background color when using the Write-Host cmdlet*

You can use both ForegroundColour and BackgroundColour together to output your desired results:

```
Write-Host "This text is displayed using foreground colour Blue and the
background
colour DarkGreen" -BackgroundColor DarkGreen -ForegroundColor Blue
```

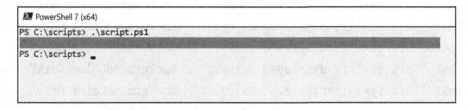

Figure 12-3. *Changing text and background colors when using the Write-Host cmdlet*

Changing the Default Console Colors

If you want to change the default text and background colors used by the console during your script, you can also set the BackgroundColor and ForegroundColour parameters. We can do it simply by using the following code:

```
$psHost = Get-Host
$window = $psHost.ui.rawui
$window.BackgroundColor = "Red"
Clear-Host
```

First, the script gets the console host and accesses the RawUI to get access to the operating system's window. From there we can set the two attributes to any of the predefined colors we have seen previously in this chapter. Calling Clear-Host will cause the console to redraw and fill it with the chosen background color. You can also set ForegroundColour so that any text written to the screen will automatically display using that color.

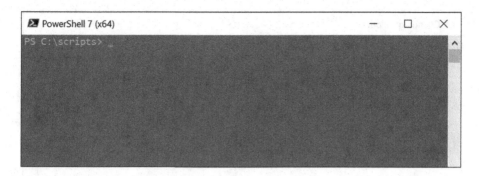

Figure 12-4. *Changing the background color of the PowerShell console*

Using this newfound knowledge, we can add these customizations to the Setup-Display function we used for the Dragon Slayer script. When setting up the display, we can now pass in the background and foreground colors.

```
function Setup-Display([string]$title, [int]$width, [int]$height,
[string]$backgroundColour, [string]$foregroundColour) {
    $psHost = Get-Host
    $window = $psHost.ui.rawui
    $newsize = $window.WindowSize
    $newsize.Height = $height
    $newsize.Width = $width
    $window.WindowSize = $newsize
    $window.WindowTitle = $title
    $window.BackgroundColor = $backgroundColour
    $window.ForegroundColor = $foregroundColour

}

Setup-Display "Changing Colours" 70 30 "Black" "Red"
Clear-Host
Write-Host "Hello this is some test text"
```

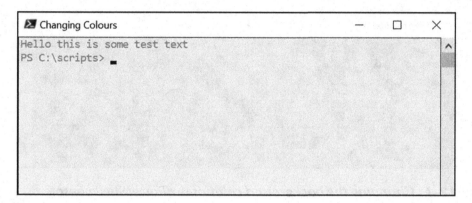

Figure 12-5. Modifying your Setup-Display function to change the text and background colors

Conclusion

Add color to highlight success or error conditions in your script or to create colorful menu systems. Make your scripts stand out, and look like a pro PowerShell guru.

CHAPTER 13

ASCII Table

Using the command line, we have access to all sorts of characters and symbols. Every character displayed on the console has a corresponding character value. All of these symbols and values can be seen on an American Standard Code for Information Interchange (ASCII) table. Since computers don't know or understand that there are different languages and since there are more languages than English in the world, there needs to be a way to represent all of the possible characters and symbols from all languages on computer systems. ASCII is how this is handled, which means that there are loads of symbols we can use and display to the console.

When building menu systems or user interfaces or while messing around writing our games for fun, we can use these hidden symbols.

Displaying Shapes and Symbols

To display a symbol from an ASCII table, you can specify a [char] type followed by its numerical value. In the following, just typing [char]120 will display the symbol associated with the numerical value 120 from the ASCII table. In this case, it displays a lowercase x:

```
[char]120
```

Figure 13-1 Shows that forcing 120 as a char object results in the x character displaying to the console. As you will see this can be very useful for creating menu systems and displaying specialised graphics to the console.

© Ian Waters 2021
I. Waters, *PowerShell for Beginners*, https://doi.org/10.1007/978-1-4842-7064-6_13

```
PowerShell 7 (x64)

PS C:\scripts> [char]120
x
PS C:\scripts> _
```

Figure 13-1. *Displaying the character value 120 to the console*

Using a quick script, we can display the first 256 symbols using a for loop and writing the numerical value and ASCII symbol using Write-Host as shown in the following:

```
for ($i = 0; $i -le 255; $i++) {
    Write-Host $i "= $([char]$i)"
}
```

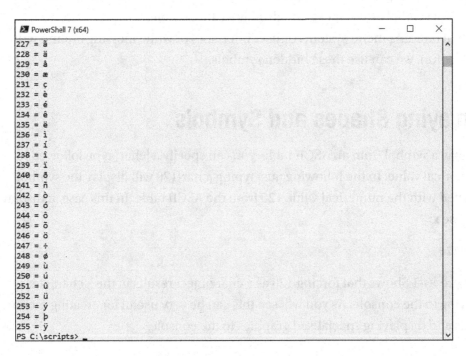

Figure 13-2. *Displaying characters using their ASCII values*

There are thousands of symbols available to use. You can increase the value in the for loop and look for any interesting symbols you can make use of.

Output an ASCII Table in HTML

I have included the following code that outputs the first 278 ASCII characters in HTML, which I used to generate the ASCII table at the end of this chapter. It gives you a sneak peek into Chapter 17 coming up later in the book. Feel free to run the code yourself and increase the value of the $showASCIITo variable to display more ASCII characters available to you to use in your own scripts.

```
#
# Outputs and ASCII table as HTML for easy viewing
#

$fileName = "ASCII Table.html"
$tableWidth = 17
$showASCIITo = 260

#Remove Existing File If It Exists
if (Test-Path $filename) {
    Remove-Item $filename
}

Add-Content $fileName "<!DOCTYPE html><html><body><style>table {border-
collapse: collapse;}
  th, td {border: 1px solid black;padding: 3px;text-align: center;}
  </style><table><tr>"

#Add Column Headers
for ($i = 0; $i -le $tableWidth; $i++) {
    if ($i % 2) {
        Add-Content $fileName "<th>Char</th>"
    }
    else {
        Add-Content $fileName "<th>Dec</th>"
    }
}
```

```
Add-Content $fileName "</tr>"

#Add Row Data
$counter = 0
for ($i = 0; $i -le (($showASCIITo / $tableWidth) * 2); $i++) {
    Add-Content $fileName "<tr>"

    for ($j = 0; $j -le $tableWidth; $j++) {
        if ($j % 2) {
            Add-Content $fileName "<td>$([char]$counter)</td>"
        }
        else {
            Add-Content $fileName "<td>$($counter)</td>"
            $counter++
        }
    }

    Add-Content $fileName "</tr>"
}
```

The ASCII table in Figure 13-3 shows the first 278 ASCII characters. The first 31 characters don't display any useful characters in the table because they are actually system characters used by very old printers. These characters signal to printers and other devices of this type what actions to perform such as go to the next line, carriage return and ring a bell, and so on.

Dec	Char	Dec	Char	Dec	Char	Dec	Char	Dec	Char	Dec	Char	Dec	Char	Dec	Char	Dec	Char
0	□	1	□	2	□	3	□	4	□	5	□	6	□	7	□	8	
9		10		11		12		13	□	14	□	15	□	16	□	17	□
18	□	19	□	20	□	21	□	22	□	23	□	24	□	25	□	26	□
27	□	28	□	29	□	30	□	31		32	!	33	"	34	#	35	$
36	%	37	&	38	'	39	(	40	)	41	*	42	+	43	,	44	-
45	.	46	/	47	0	48	1	49	2	50	3	51	4	52	5	53	6
54	7	55	8	56	9	57	:	58	;	59	<	60	=	61	>	62	?
63	@	64	A	65	B	66	C	67	D	68	E	69	F	70	G	71	H
72	I	73	J	74	K	75	L	76	M	77	N	78	O	79	P	80	Q
81	R	82	S	83	T	84	U	85	V	86	W	87	X	88	Y	89	Z
90	[	91	\	92	]	93	^	94	_	95	`	96	a	97	b	98	c
99	d	100	e	101	f	102	g	103	h	104	i	105	j	106	k	107	l
108	m	109	n	110	o	111	p	112	q	113	r	114	s	115	t	116	u
117	v	118	w	119	x	120	y	121	z	122	{	123	|	124	}	125	~
126		127	?	128	□	129	?	130	?	131	?	132	?	133	?	134	?
135	?	136	?	137	?	138	?	139	?	140	□	141	?	142	□	143	□
144	?	145	?	146	?	147	?	148	?	149	?	150	?	151	?	152	?
153	?	154	?	155	?	156	□	157	?	158	?	159		160	¡	161	¢
162	£	163	¤	164	¥	165	¦	166	§	167	¨	168	©	169	ª	170	«
171	¬	172		173	®	174	¯	175	°	176	±	177	²	178	³	179	´
180	µ	181	¶	182	·	183	¸	184	¹	185	º	186	»	187	¼	188	½
189	¾	190	¿	191	À	192	Á	193	Â	194	Ã	195	Ä	196	Å	197	Æ
198	Ç	199	È	200	É	201	Ê	202	Ë	203	Ì	204	Í	205	Î	206	Ï
207	Ð	208	Ñ	209	Ò	210	Ó	211	Ô	212	Õ	213	Ö	214	×	215	Ø
216	Ù	217	Ú	218	Û	219	Ü	220	Ý	221	Þ	222	ß	223	à	224	á
225	â	226	ã	227	ä	228	å	229	æ	230	ç	231	è	232	é	233	ê
234	ë	235	ì	236	í	237	î	238	ï	239	ð	240	ñ	241	ò	242	ó
243	ô	244	õ	245	ö	246	÷	247	ø	248	ù	249	ú	250	û	251	ü
252	ý	253	þ	254	ÿ	255	A	256	a	257	A	258	a	259	A	260	a
261	C	262	c	263	C	264	c	265	C	266	c	267	C	268	c	269	D
270	d	271	Đ	272	d	273	E	274	e	275	E	276	e	277	E	278	e

Figure 13-3. *Example ASCII table*

Building a Menu Box

One use for these hidden characters is to make your scripts look a little more professional by using boxes around your menu systems. If you expand the number of characters displayed using the code earlier in this chapter, you will find some nice box-looking characters:

╡ ║ ╗ ╝ ╚ ╔ ╩ ╦ ╠ ═ ╬

131

To write out these characters into Visual Studio Code, hold down the left Alt key and type 185 and let go. These characters range from 185 to 206. Have a go yourself and see what hidden characters you can find.

Using these, you can build out a nice menu system like this, which looks a lot more professional:

```
╔══════════════════════════════════════════════════╗
║   Menu System                                      ║
╠══════════════════════════════════════════════════╣
║   Press 1 to select option 1                       ║
║   Press 2 to select option 2                       ║
║   Press 3 to select option 3                       ║
║   Press 4 to select option 4                       ║
╚══════════════════════════════════════════════════╝
```

Conclusion

ASCII tables were used heavily back in the day, and text-based games made good use of many of the hidden symbols to build levels and menu systems on the screen. Use them to enhance the professional look of your own scripts to set your work apart from the rest.

CHAPTER 14

Cursor Control

Now this is where I think the fun really begins! If you are going to write some fun little games using PowerShell, then we need to move the cursor around and draw characters and other objects on the display at different locations.

Moving the Cursor

Let's start by writing a small function to move the cursor to a position within the console window. To specify the location, we will use the typical X and Y map coordinates. In the Windows operating system, the 0,0 location specifies the top-left corner of the display, that is, the first character position within the window.

To move the cursor, we can access the host variable and the RawUI controls as we have done previously. Under RawUI, we can access the CursorPosition variable and set a new value by passing it an X and Y value as a Coordinates variable type.

In the following script, we define the Move-Cursor function with two required parameters, x and y. The script clears the console display, then moves to a set location, and writes an X to the display.

Note here we need to set the -NoNewLine optional parameter so that the Write-Host cmdlet doesn't move the cursor to the next line. We want to control the cursor's location from now on!

```
function Move-Cursor([int]$x, [int] $y) {
    $host.UI.RawUI.CursorPosition = New-Object System.Management.
    Automation.Host.Coordinates $x , $y
}
```

© Ian Waters 2021
I. Waters, *PowerShell for Beginners*, https://doi.org/10.1007/978-1-4842-7064-6_14

```
Clear-Host
Move-Cursor 5 2
Write-Host "X" -NoNewLine
Move-Cursor 10 4
Write-Host "X" -NoNewLine
Move-Cursor 30 6
Write-Host "X" -NoNewLine
Move-Cursor 20 5
Write-Host "X" -NoNewLine
```

If you run the code, you will see the cursor moves to the specified positions and writes an X at those positions as shown in Figure 14-1.

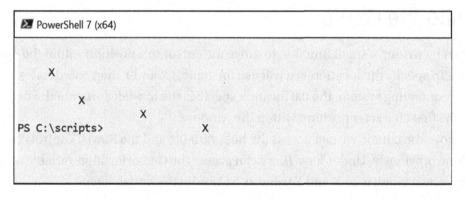

Figure 14-1. *Displaying text at different positions in the PowerShell console*

Ok, now just for fun, let's use our newfound power to create a star field effect on the screen. In the following, I've written a little script to display an X on the screen in 20 different and random locations. Using the built-in cmdlet Get-Random, we can request a random value to use for the X and Y positions. Get-Random has a few optional parameters we can pass it to restrict the values it returns. Using -Minimum and -Maximum, we can set the star field to start at position 0,0 and have a maximum size of 120 characters wide and 25 characters high.

```
function Setup-Display([string]$title, [int]$width, [int]$height) {
    $psHost = Get-Host
    $window = $psHost.ui.rawui
    $newsize = $window.WindowSize
    $newsize.Height = $height
    $newsize.Width = $width
    $window.WindowSize = $newsize
    $window.WindowTitle = $title
}

function Move-Cursor([int]$x, [int] $y) {
    $host.UI.RawUI.CursorPosition = New-Object System.Management.
    Automation.Host.Coordinates $x , $y
}

Clear-Host
Setup-Display "Move Cursor Demo" 120 25

#Loop 20 times and display an X in a random location
For ($i = 0; $i -lt 20; $i++) {

    #Generate random values for the X and Y positions
    $x = Get-Random -Minimum 0 -Maximum 119
    $y = Get-Random -Minimum 0 -Maximum 24

    #Move to the random location
    Move-Cursor $x $y

    #Display an X and disable a new line character
    Write-Host "X" -NoNewline
}

#Move to cursor to the bottom of the display
Move-Cursor 0 31
```

Figure 14-2 shows the star field effect created by this script. Having the ability to move the cursor around the console windows opens up the possibility for us to create some fun little games in later chapters.

Figure 14-2. *Creating a star field using the Move-Cursor function you created*

Moving a Character Around the Screen

Now that we have added another new function to our pool of code, we are now in a position to write a script that can set up the display to our requirements, read key presses, and draw objects to the screen in positions we want.

Keeping Within the Boundaries

There are a couple of code snippets I wanted to highlight for you, which may be of some interest. In the code, we need a way to stop the player or other objects from going off the edge of the console window display area. If they were to move outside of the console window, the script would throw an error because you can't write output to an area outside of it. What we do in the following code is use some basic if else if statements to look at the position of the player. If their current X position is less than 0, we set it back to 0, which keeps the player from moving off the left side of the console window. In the else if statement, we calculate if the X position of the character goes past the right-hand side of the console window. If it does, we set the position back to the display width – the character width. We then do the same for the top and bottom of the screen to keep them within the console window boundary:

```powershell
#Keep player inside the display
    if ($xPosition -le 0) {
        $xPosition = 0
    }
    elseif ($xPosition -ge $displayWidth - $characterWidth) {
        $xPosition = $displayWidth - $characterWidth
    }

    if ($yPosition -le 0) {
        $yPosition = 0
    }
    elseif ($yPosition -ge $displayHeight - $characterHeight) {
        $yPosition = $displayHeight - $characterHeight
    }
```

Reducing the Flicker

Another section of code I wanted to highlight is used to reduce the amount of flickering on the screen. We do this by only drawing the character on the screen if the character has moved positions. If you were to remove it, the character would constantly flicker, which is annoying and looks horrible. The reason for the flicker is that we need to clear the console screen and move the cursor around the screen. PowerShell is not really meant for this type of things, but we are learning and it's fun, so its ok. ☺ Later on in the book, I'll show you a method for further reducing the screen flicker issue:

```powershell
#Only draw display if there is an update
if ($update) {
    Clear-Host
    Draw-Character
    $update = $false
}
```

Bring It All Together

Ok, let's tie everything together into a script that will form the basis of a PowerShell game where a player can move characters around the screen and move through levels. Take some time to follow through the code and run the code example yourself to help you fully understand how it works. Why not design your own character and modify the code to work without any errors when trying to move off the sides of the console window?

```
#Variables###########
[bool]$done = $false
[int]$xPosition = 0
[int]$yPosition = 0
[bool]$update = $true
[int]$displayWidth = 110
[int]$displayHeight = 55
[int]$characterHeight = 4
[int]$characterWidth = 4
#####################

#Functions####################################################################
function Setup-Display([string]$title, [int]$width, [int]$height) {
    $psHost = get-host
    $window = $psHost.ui.rawui
    $newsize = $window.WindowSize
    $newsize.Height = $height
    $newsize.Width = $width
    $window.WindowSize = $newsize
    $window.WindowTitle = $title
}

function Move-Cursor([int]$x, [int] $y) {
    $host.UI.RawUI.CursorPosition = New-Object System.Management.
    Automation.Host.Coordinates $x , $y
}
```

```powershell
function Read-Character() {
    if ($host.ui.RawUI.KeyAvailable) {
        return $Host.UI.RawUI.ReadKey("NoEcho,IncludeKeyDown").Character
    }

    return $null
}

function Draw-Character() {
    Move-Cursor $xPosition $yPosition
    write-host "####"
    Move-Cursor $xPosition ($yPosition + 1)
    write-host "#  #"
    Move-Cursor $xPosition ($yPosition + 2)
    write-host "#  #"
    Move-Cursor $xPosition ($yPosition + 3)
    write-host "####"
    Move-Cursor 0 0
}
############################################################################

#Start Running Program Commands

#Clear screen
Clear-Host

Setup-Display "Move Character" $displayWidth $displayHeight

while (!$done) {
    #See what keys the player is pressing
    $char = Read-Character

    if ($char -eq 'q') {
        $done = $true
        $update = $true
    }
    elseif ($char -eq 'a') {
        $xPosition--
        $update = $true
    }
```

```
    elseif ($char -eq 'd') {
        $xPosition++
        $update = $true
    }
    elseif ($char -eq 's') {
        $yPosition++
        $update = $true
    }
    elseif ($char -eq 'w') {
        $yPosition--
        $update = $true
    }

    #Keep player inside the display
    if ($xPosition -le 0) {
        $xPosition = 0
    }
    elseif ($xPosition -ge $displayWidth - $characterWidth) {
        $xPosition = $displayWidth - $characterWidth
    }

    if ($yPosition -le 0) {
        $yPosition = 0
    }
    elseif ($yPosition -ge $displayHeight - $characterHeight) {
        $yPosition = $displayHeight - $characterHeight
    }

    #Only draw display if there is an update
    if ($update) {
        Clear-Host
        Draw-Character
        $update = $false
    }
}

#Clear screen
Clear-Host
```

Run the script and press A to move left, D to move right, S to move down, and W to move up. You will notice that the screen flickers while moving, and this is because we are directly drawing to the display during each frame. There is a trick to solving the screen flicker problem, which we will explore in a later chapter.

Figure 14-3 shows the box on the screen. Run the code yourself and move it around. We are one step closer to writing a small game with moving characters!

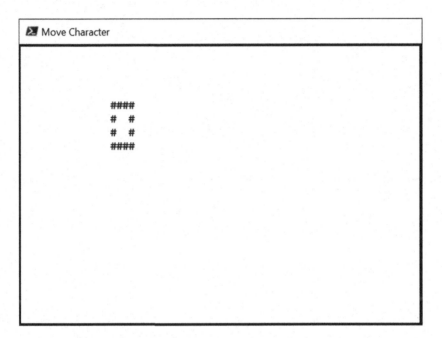

Figure 14-3. *Moving your first game object around the screen*

Conclusion

This was quite an exciting chapter and the first time we have really seen how we can start writing cool little PowerShell games. Play around with the source code yourself and design your own characters to move around.

Background Processing

If you ever need to run a task in the background or have multiple smaller tasks that you want to run in parallel, you can use PowerShell jobs. Jobs are blocks of code that run in their own PowerShell instance, and you can retrieve the output at any point and even stop the job when required. Let's say you need to write a script that needs to connect to all computers on a network and retrieve their operating system version to build a report. Doing this task individually could take a very long time, but if you could run ten of these tasks at once, you can greatly reduce the overall amount of time that report would take to run. I do this type of task along with others such as connecting to multiple Microsoft and Google cloud services to retrieve report information for our business clients. Running the tasks as individual background jobs takes a fraction of the time.

Starting a Job

To spawn a job, you first need to define a script block, which is essentially a small script, which will be passed into the Start-Job cmdlet. You can also set up as many parameters as you wish, which can be passed into the script block from the cmdlet when it's created.

In the following, we define the script block and set up a parameter $countTo. The rest of the script is a for loop that will count from 0 up to the parameter value. To start the job, we simply need to call Start-Job and pass in the script block and use the -ArgumentList parameter to pass in the parameters required for the script block.

© Ian Waters 2021
I. Waters, *PowerShell for Beginners*, https://doi.org/10.1007/978-1-4842-7064-6_15

```
$scriptBlock =
{
    param($countTo)

    for ($i = 0; $i -le $countTo; $i++) {
        Write-Host "Counter:$i"
        Start-Sleep -Seconds 1
    }
}

Start-Job $scriptBlock -ArgumentList 100
```

As shown in Figure 15-1, we call the script, and it returns the details of the job, which includes the job ID that is used to uniquely identity this particular job. You will need this ID to call other job cmdlets later on in your code. You can also view the state of the script, if it is running, stopped, suspended, or completed. The final useful information is the HasMoreData variable. This tells you if there is any information available to be collected from the job.

Notice in Figure 15-1 that we can get the status of all jobs or jobs with a specific state using the cmdlet Get-Job. Passing in the optional parameter -State, you can return only "Running" jobs.

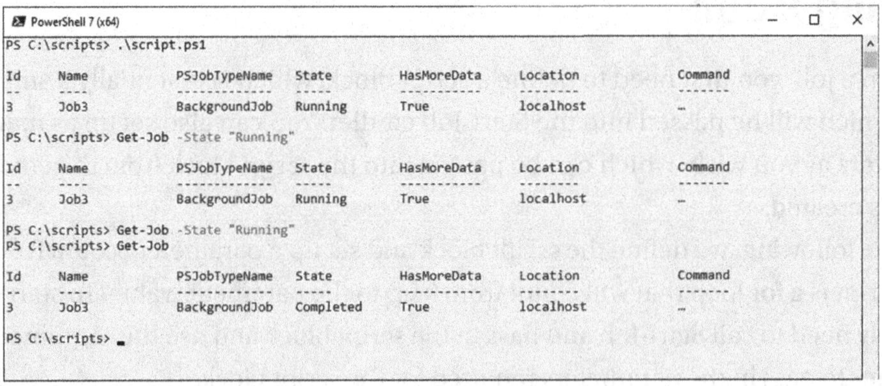

Figure 15-1. *Retrieving background jobs and their status*

Managing a Specific Job and Passing Multiple Parameters

After a while, your scripts may generate multiple jobs, which will be in various states. We can call the Get-Job cmdlet to return a list of all jobs. In Figure 15-2, you can see that there is two Running jobs and one Completed.

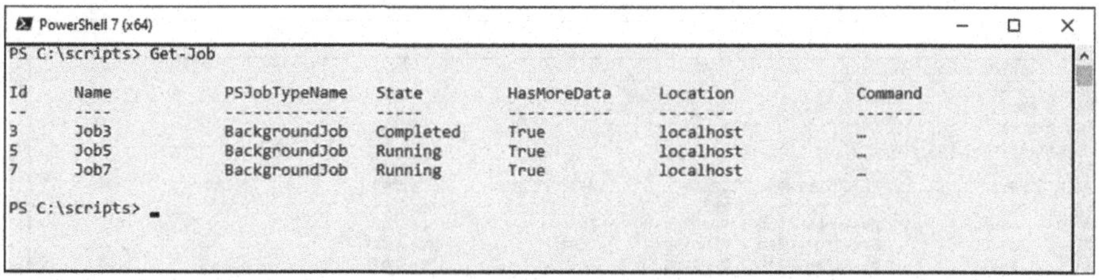

Figure 15-2. *Using Get-Job to return all jobs on the system*

When you start a job, you can retrieve a reference to the job and use that to capture its ID. This is very useful when spawning multiple jobs; you could even add jobs to an ArrayList to keep track of them.

In the following is a modified version of the previous script. This time we define two parameters $countFrom and $countTo, and we also save the details of the jobs to separate variables $job1, $job2, and $job3.

```
$scriptBlock =
{
    param($countFrom, $countTo)

    for ($i = 0; $i -le $countTo; $i++) {
        Write-Host "Counter:$i"
        Start-Sleep -Seconds 1
    }
}

$job1 = Start-Job $scriptBlock -ArgumentList 50, 100
$job2 = Start-Job $scriptBlock -ArgumentList 0, 100
$job3 = Start-Job $scriptBlock -ArgumentList 20, 100
```

```
Write-Host "Job 1 id:$($job1.Id)"
Write-Host "Job 2 id:$($job2.Id)"
Write-Host "Job 3 id:$($job3.Id)"
```

Now that we have captured the job details after creating them, we can more accurately track and work with them later in our scripts. See in Figure 15-3 the ID and name listed for the spawned jobs.

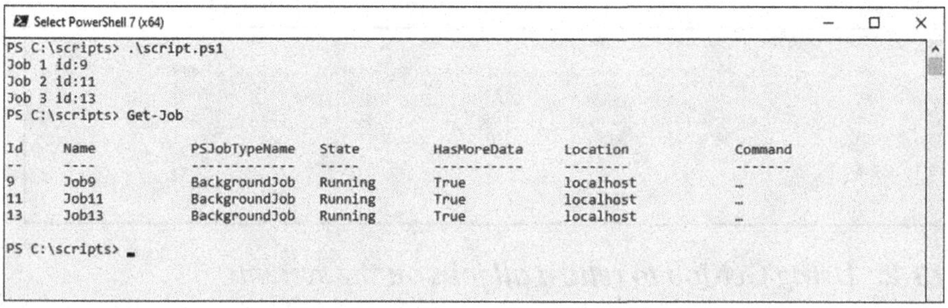

Figure 15-3. *Getting background job IDs*

Receiving the Results of a Job

When you run a job in the background, you may want to retrieve its output to keep track of its progress or capture the results of its progress while it's still running. To do this, we can use the cmdlet Receive-Job and pass in the id as a parameter of the job we want to receive the output from.

In the following, we run the previous script that outputs the IDs of the three jobs created. We then call Receive-Job and pass in the ID of the first job created. The output from that cmdlet is then output to the console. The script block uses the cmdlet Write-Output to output the progress of its counting. Each time we call Receive-Job, it returns new output. Nice. Each time the cmdlet is called, only new output is returned, never the complete list. This is useful as it means we can constantly retrieve new updates from the job as it progresses.

Figure 15-4 shows me calling Receive-Job to get updated output from different jobs.

```
PowerShell 7 (x64)                                     —   □   ×
PS C:\scripts> .\script.ps1
Job 1 id:27
Job 2 id:29
Job 3 id:31
PS C:\scripts> Receive-Job -id 27
Counter:0
Counter:1
Counter:2
Counter:3
Counter:4
PS C:\scripts> Receive-Job -id 29
Counter:0
Counter:1
Counter:2
Counter:3
Counter:4
Counter:5
Counter:6
Counter:7
PS C:\scripts> Receive-Job -id 31
Counter:0
Counter:1
Counter:2
Counter:3
Counter:4
Counter:5
Counter:6
Counter:7
Counter:8
Counter:9
Counter:10
PS C:\scripts> Receive-Job -id 31
Counter:11
Counter:12
Counter:13
Counter:14
Counter:15
Counter:16
Counter:17
Counter:18
Counter:19
Counter:20
Counter:21
PS C:\scripts> _
```

Figure 15-4. *Using Receive-Job to retrieve the output from background jobs*

The cmdlet Receive-Job is returning an array of string values. We can capture the new output into a variable and process the output in our script as required:

```
$results = Receive-Job -Job $job1

foreach ($res in $results) {
    Write-Host $res
}
```

Stopping Jobs

If you need to stop a job in its tracks, simply call the cmdlet Stop-Job and pass in the ID of the job you wish to stop. You might want to do this if you detect an error or need to restart a task from the beginning. Using my example from the beginning of this chapter, you may write a script that scans a network and retrieves information from all computers on the network. Well, if a user runs the script with the wrong input parameters, they may want to stop the existing report and run it again with the correct parameters. If you don't stop and remove jobs, they will continue to take up system resources. We will cover removing stopped jobs in the next section.

Here is a modified version of our script again; and this time it creates a job, gets its status, and stops the job and then retrieves its status again.

Note that once a job has been stopped, it cannot be resumed or started again.

```
$scriptBlock =
{
    param($countFrom, $countTo)

    for ($i = 0; $i -le $countTo; $i++) {
        Write-output "Counter:$i"
        Start-Sleep -Seconds 1
    }
}

Write-Host "Starting Job"

$job = Start-Job $scriptBlock -ArgumentList 0, 100

Write-Host "Job Started ID:$($job.Id)"

Write-Host "Getting Job Status"
Get-Job -id $job.Id

Write-Host "Stopping Job"
Stop-Job -Id $job.Id

Write-Host "Getting Job Status"
Get-Job -id $job.Id
```

Figure 15-5 shows the output from the script. A stop is started then Stop-Job is used to hault the background process.

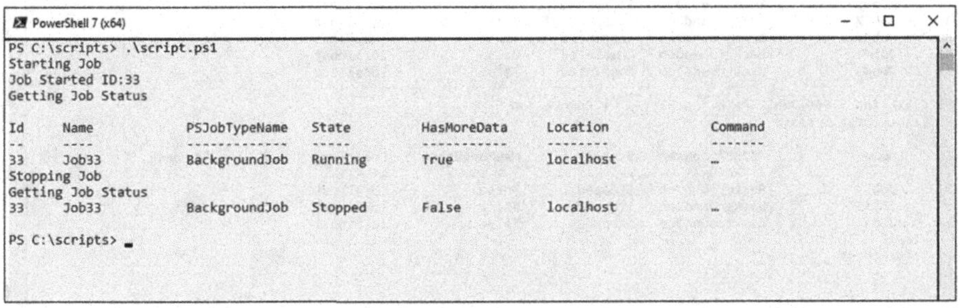

Figure 15-5. *Stopping a background job*

Removing Jobs

Once your script is finished or if you have a long-running script, you may want to remove stopped and completed jobs. Leaving jobs in a stopped or completed state can use up system resources, so it's best to remove jobs that are no longer needed. To do this, simply call the cmdlet Remove-Job and pass in the ID of the job. If you want to remove all completed jobs, you can call Get-Job and pass the output directly into Remove-Job as shown in the following:

```
Remove-Job -id $job.Id
```

```
Get-Job -Status "Completed" | Remove-Job
```

Figure 15-6 shows running Remove-Job to clear all completed jobs freeing up system resources for other tasks.

```
PowerShell 7 (x64)                                                              —   □   ×

PS C:\scripts> Get-Job

Id    Name     PSJobTypeName    State      HasMoreData    Location    Command
--    ----     -------------    -----      -----------    --------    -------
33    Job33    BackgroundJob    Stopped    False          localhost   …
35    Job35    BackgroundJob    Stopped    False          localhost   …
37    Job37    BackgroundJob    Stopped    False          localhost   …
39    Job39    BackgroundJob    Completed  False          localhost   …
41    Job41    BackgroundJob    Completed  False          localhost   …
43    Job43    BackgroundJob    Completed  False          localhost   …

PS C:\scripts> Get-Job -State "Completed" | Remove-Job
PS C:\scripts> Get-Job

Id    Name     PSJobTypeName    State      HasMoreData    Location    Command
--    ----     -------------    -----      -----------    --------    -------
33    Job33    BackgroundJob    Stopped    False          localhost   …
35    Job35    BackgroundJob    Stopped    False          localhost   …
37    Job37    BackgroundJob    Stopped    False          localhost   …

PS C:\scripts> _
```

Figure 15-6. Removing completed jobs using the Remove-Job cmdlet

Conclusion

Jobs are a great way of running multiple short jobs in the background. In a game, you could use a job to control a character or object in the level; and in a utility script, you could use a job to retrieve information from lots of computers on the network in one go and monitor the results of each job until they all complete.

It's worth noting that jobs are great but remember each job runs in its own PowerShell session, so they can't interact with variables defined in the calling script. Each job must be able to act on its own independently from the calling script.

CHAPTER 16

Networking

Even in PowerShell scripts, we have some pretty awesome network functionality especially since we can leverage the .Net framework and all of its helper objects. We can write scripts to open ports, connect to them, and send and receive messages. Writing a multiplayer game in PowerShell would certainly prove your knowledge and make all of your colleagues jealous of your ninja skills. In this chapter, we are going to start by writing a very simple server script that will open a port and listen for new connections and pick up new messages it receives. We will then write a client script that will read a line of input from the user and send it to the server script to be displayed to the console. From these basic beginnings, you will have the foundations to write any networking script you require from a small web server or chat messaging system through to multiplayer games.

Basic Networking Introduction

Networking is a complex subject to cover, but for this chapter all you will need to know is that computers on a network talk to each other using different protocols. Protocols outline how computers talk to each other, and some offer error checking and reconnection functionality, and one of the most used protocols for computer networks is the Transmission Control Protocol (TCP). If we set up a TCP connection to another computer, the protocol will handle the details of getting our messages to the correct destination.

The computer program listening for connections is called the server, and the program making the connection is referred to as the client.

When a computer wants to start listening for connections, it opens up a port and waits for a client to connect to it on that specified port number. Ports are like letterboxes in a block of flats. There are usually a number of letterboxes, and letters are delivered into the correct letterbox and end up in the correct flat. Think of each flat as a specific computer program.

© Ian Waters 2021
I. Waters, *PowerShell for Beginners*, https://doi.org/10.1007/978-1-4842-7064-6_16

The idea is similar in the computer networking world. A block of flats represents a computer, and the individual flats represent individual programs running on the computer. If you want to send a message to a server, you need to know its network address, and you also need to know the port number to be able to talk to the correct server program.

Web pages talk over TCP ports 80 and 443. If you load up a web browser and type google.com into the address bar, the browser knows that you want to connect to the address "google.com" on port 80 if using http or port 443 if you use https.

In the example in this chapter, we will connect to the local computer on port 2000. We will set up a server to listen on port 2000 and a client script that will connect to port 2000 and send and receive messages.

Creating a Basic Server App

A server script needs to start a listener, which is an object that listens for client applications connecting. Once a client has connected, we then need to create a gateway or tunnel through which we can send and receive messages.

Creating the Listener

To allow our script to receive messages from clients on the network, we first need to create a System.Net.IPEndPoint object. This defines what IP address and port number our script will be using to receive messages on the network. Second, we need to create a .NET listener object, which will wait for clients to connect on the specified IP address and port number.

In this example, we set the port number to 2000, but you can choose any port number you wish. In networking, the first 1024 ports are reserved for well-known and established network services, so it's best to choose a number above this range.

```
$port = 2000
$endPoint = new-object System.Net.IPEndPoint ([system.net.ipaddress]::any, $port)
$listener = new-object System.Net.Sockets.TcpListener $endPoint
$listener.start()
$client = $listener.AcceptTcpClient()
```

Once we have a client connected to our server service, we need to open up a stream/connection through which they can exchange messages with each other. Then we can use the .NET object System.IO.StreamReader to handle the reading of new messages from the stream:

```
$stream = $client.GetStream()
```

Reading New Messages

Now that we have a .NET System.IO.StreamReader object, we can read lines of text sent through the stream using the ReadLine method. ReadLine will return null if there is no data to be read or a string containing the characters. We can save the text into a variable and decide what to do with it in your script. In this example, we are simply going to write the received text out to the console:

```
$reader = New-Object System.IO.StreamReader $stream

$line = ""

while ($line -ne "QUIT") {
    $line = $reader.ReadLine()

    if ($line -ne $null) {
        Write-Host "Message Recieved:" $line
    }
}
```

Ok, now let's put everything together to create the server script.

```
Clear-Host
$port = 2000
$endPoint = new-object System.Net.IPEndPoint ([system.net.ipaddress]::any,
$port)
$listener = new-object System.Net.Sockets.TcpListener $endPoint
$listener.Start()

Write-Host "Server Running"
```

```
$client = $listener.AcceptTcpClient()

Write-Host "Client Connected"

$stream = $client.GetStream();
$reader = New-Object System.IO.StreamReader $stream
$line = ""

while ($line -ne "QUIT") {
    $line = $reader.ReadLine()
    if ($line -ne $null) {
        Write-Host "Message Recieved:" $line
    }
}

Write-Host "Shutting Down"

$reader.Dispose()
$stream.Dispose()
$client.Dispose()
$listener.Stop()
```

Creating a Basic Client App

A client app makes a connection to a server, and in our example, we need a separate
script to run as the client. Let's build a simple client app that will connect to the server
and use a .NET System.IO.StreamWriter object to send messages to the server script.

Creating the TCP Client

To create the client app, we first create a .Net TcpClient object and pass in the port
number and server name. In this example, we use the server name "localhost." All
Windows-based computers can refer to themselves as localhost to make connections
to themselves. If you wanted to run the server script on another computer, you would
need to set the $server variable to the name or IP address of the other computer. In this
example, we will be running both scripts on the same computer, so we can connect to
the server using "localhost" to make it easier to get started:

```
$port = 2000
$server = "localhost"
$client = New-Object System.Net.Sockets.TcpClient $server, $port
```

Sending Messages

Once we have a client connected to our server service, we need to open up a stream/
connection through which they can exchange messages with each other. Then we can
use the .Net object System.IO.StreamWriter to handle the sending of new messages
through the stream:

```
$stream = $client.GetStream()
$writer = New-Object System.IO.StreamWriter $stream
$writer.AutoFlush = $true

do {
    $message = Read-Host -prompt "Send Message"
    $writer.WriteLine($message)

}
while ($message -notlike "QUIT")
```

Putting It All Together

Now we can put all of this code together into a client script. The script will connect
to the server and continually read a line from the keyboard and send the line via the
StreamWriter object. If the user types QUIT, the script stops looping and disposes of the
resources used.

```
Clear-Host

$port = 2000
$server = "localhost"
$client = New-Object System.Net.Sockets.TcpClient $server, $port
$stream = $client.GetStream()
$writer = New-Object System.IO.StreamWriter $stream
$writer.AutoFlush = $true
```

```
do {
    $message = Read-Host -prompt "Send Message"
    $writer.WriteLine($message)
}
while ($message -notlike "QUIT")

$writer.Dispose()
$stream.Dispose()
$client.Dispose()
```

Save both scripts individually and open two PowerShell consoles. Run the server script in the first and then run the client script in the second.

If all works correctly, you will be able to type messages into the client script console and press Enter to send them to the server. The server console will then display the messages.

When you start the server script, you may be prompted to allow the program to connect through the firewall. Since the script opens port 2000, the firewall needs to allow port 2000 to be accessed by the client. If you can't get the scripts to work, it's likely that your firewall is blocking port 2000.

Figure 16-1 shows running the server and client scripts together. The server is waiting for a connection and lists "Client Connected" when the client script in Figure 16-2 connects to it. I then enter some text, and after pressing Enter, it is sent to the server script and displayed to the console.

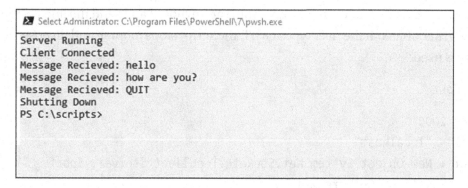

Figure 16-1. *Running the network server script*

> Administrator: C:\Program Files\PowerShell\7\pwsh.exe
>
> ```
> Send Message: hello
> Send Message: how are you?
> Send Message: QUIT
> PS C:\scripts>
> ```

Figure 16-2. *Running the network client script and sending text to the server*

Conclusion

Being able to implement network functionality within your scripts opens up a world of possibilities. Connecting to networked services and combining the power of automation, you can push yourself into the realms of an advanced PowerShell coder!

CHAPTER 17

Working with Files

Using a few PowerShell cmdlets and even some built-in tricks, we can read from and write to files. This is especially useful if you write a script that gets run multiple times and you need to save data or script options to retrieve at a later date. You may also want to save data collected from a script into a CSV file, which could later be imported into Excel to produce a report. For us, we can use basic text files to store level, character, and other object graphics and settings. We can even store character scripts, which control movement and behavior by loading the code into our main scripts. We will look at how to do that later in the book, but for now let's learn a few basics and at the end write code to load levels, characters, and other objects.

Checking If a File Exists

If you're going to read or write to a file, it's a good idea to check it exists first. Most cmdlets will return some sort of error if they can't find the file they're looking to work with, but there are times when you just want to check if a file exists or not. One reason may be that your script behaves differently if a configuration file has not been created yet. If it's not found, then you may want to run through some initial setup procedure. If the file does exist, then you know the setup has been completed, and you can skip the setup steps in your script.

```
Clear-Host

#Save file name and path to a variable
$file = "c:\scripts\testfile.txt"

#Call Test-Path cmdlet and pass in the full file path
#It will return $True if the file exists and $False if not
$fileExists = Test-Path $file
```

© Ian Waters 2021
I. Waters, *PowerShell for Beginners*, https://doi.org/10.1007/978-1-4842-7064-6_17

```
#Test if the $fileExists variable is true which means the file does exist
if ($fileExists -eq $True) {
    Write-Host "c:\scripts\Testfile.txt exists"
}else {
    Write-Host "c:\scripts\Testfile.txt does not exist"
}
```

In Figure 17-1, I have my script and test file in the Scripts directory.

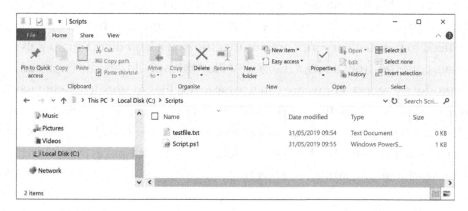

Figure 17-1. *Creating a testfile.txt text file*

Now if we run the script as shown in Figure 17-2, the script reports that the file exists because Test-Path $file returns $true, and the code in the if statement runs.

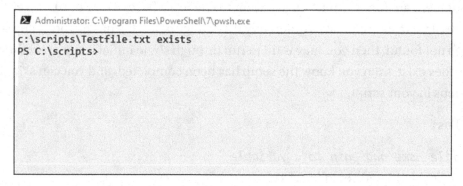

Figure 17-2. *Using the Test-Path cmdlet to see if a file exists*

If I now delete the testfile.txt file and rerun the script as shown in Figure 17-3, it now reports that the file does not exist because Test-Path returns $false, resulting in a different path through the code.

```
Administrator: C:\Program Files\PowerShell\7\pwsh.exe

c:\scripts\Testfile.txt does not exist
PS C:\scripts>
```

Figure 17-3. *Using Test-Path cmdlet to test if a file does not exist in the specified location*

Reading Files

Reading text files is easy using the Get-Content cmdlet. Pass this cmdlet a path to the text file, and it will read all of the contents of the file and return an array of string values. You can then access the elements in the array as usual, by directly accessing them using, for example, $lines[0] to read the first line or by using a for or foreach loop.

In the following script, we first check to see if the file exists and if it does read the content of the file. We then use a foreach loop to display each line from the file. If the file doesn't exist, then we display a message to the user.

First, open the test file and add some lines to it so that the text will display to the console and then run the script.

```
#Clear the console
Clear-Host

#Save full file path to variable
$filePath = "c:\scripts\testfile.txt"

#Check if file exists
$fileExists = Test-Path $filePath

if ($fileExists -eq $True) {
    #Read lines in one go and access lines
    $lines = Get-Content $filePath
```

```
    Write-Host "Number of lines in the file:" $lines.Count

    #Loop throught the $lines array of string values
    Foreach ($line in $lines) {
        Write-Host $line
    }
}else {
    Write-Host "$filePath is missing"
}
```

In this code, you can see that Get-Content is used to return an array of strings, and we store them into the $lines variable. We then use a foreach loop to loop through all entries in the array and write each line out to the console as shown in Figure 17-4.

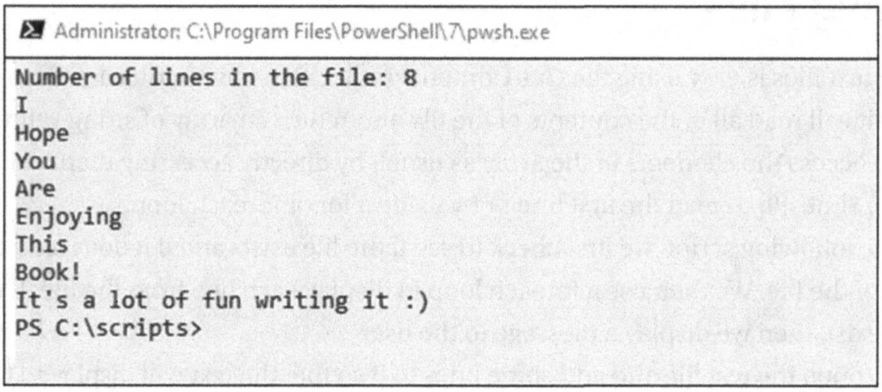

Figure 17-4. *Using the Get-Content cmdlet to read a text file*

Writing to Files

Writing to files is easy using a couple of simple cmdlets.

Add-Content can be used to create a file if it doesn't exist, but if it does, it will add text to the end of it.

We will also look at using Set-Content, which will also create a file if it doesn't exist, only this time if there is already an existing file, it overwrites that file with an empty one removing the existing contents.

Both use the same set of parameters. We use -Path to specify the location and name of the file and -Value to pass in a single line or an array of string values.

Add-Content

In the following script, we use Add-Content to add the specified strings in the $fileContent array to the end of the file. If the file doesn't exist, it will first create one and then add the content to it. Give this a try yourself and run the code multiple times and see what happens.

```
#Clear the console
Clear-Host
```

```
#File content
$fileContent = @("Line 1", "Line 2", "Line 3")
```

```
#Save full file path to variable
$filePath = "c:\scripts\testfile.txt"
```

```
Add-Content -Path $filePath -Value $fileContent
```

```
Write-Host "File has been created and the new file content has been added to it."
```

Let's start by running the script with no file present at the specified location, so remove any existing testfile.txt file in the Scripts folder first.

The first time the script runs, it prompts that the file has been created and the contents passed to it have been added to the file as shown in Figure 17-5.

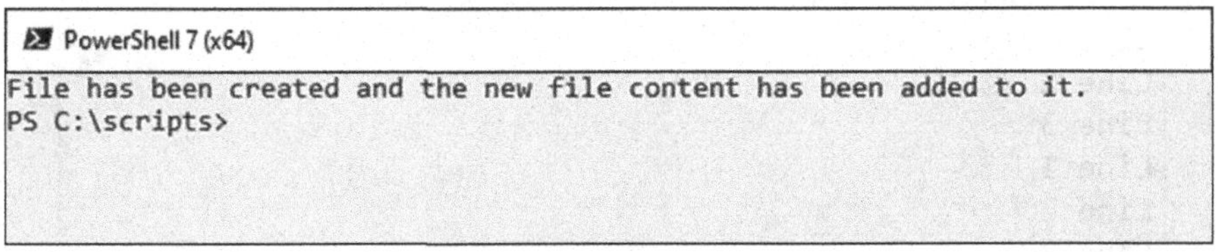

Figure 17-5. *Using the Add-Content cmdlet to create a text file and write to it*

We can see in the specified location the file has been created and the file contains the example text specified in the array as shown in Figure 17-6.

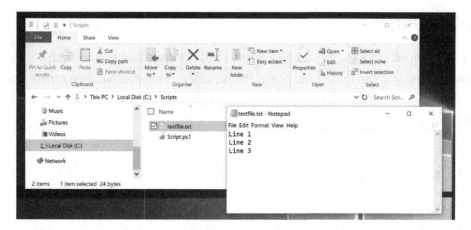

Figure 17-6. *Text file showing how the script has written multiple lines to it*

Now if you run the script a second time, Add-Content detects the existing file and appends the example text from the array to the end of it. See that the example text has been appended to the end of the file leaving what was there already intact.

If we run the script again it will add lines to the end of the file. This can be useful when writing log files where you want to keep the previous contents of the file and simply add some new information. Figure 17-7 shows the contents of textfile.txt after running the script twice.

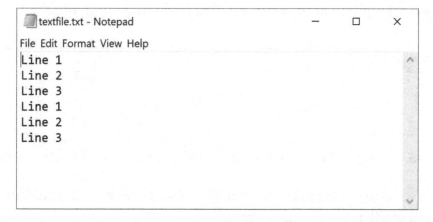

Figure 17-7. *Text file showing how Add-Content added multiple new lines*

Set-Content

Now let's modify the code to use Set-Content instead, and running this code the first time will create the testfile.txt file if it doesn't exist. The difference this time is that no matter how many times you run the script, the contents remain the same. Give it a try for yourself and see.

```
#Clear the console
Clear-Host

#File content
$fileContent = @("Line 1", "Line 2", "Line 3")

#Save full file path to variable
$filePath = "c:\scripts\testfile.txt"

Set-Content -Path $filePath -Value $fileContent

Write-Host "File has been created or overwritten and the new file content
has been added to it."
```

Conclusion

Reading and writing to plaintext files is easy using PowerShell cmdlets and a great option for setting up configuration files to save user preferences. They are also a good option to use as a basic way to log script errors or progress for later review.

CHAPTER 18

Sound

If we are going to spend some time writing a game using PowerShell, then we better make it sound good. Old-school classic kinda good! Playing basic beeps at different pitches for different lengths of time or using the .Net framework and utilizing the Speech or SoundPlayer class to get more immersive and advanced.

Beep, Beep

For playing basic beep sounds, you can use [console]::beep(659, 500).

Pass the beep function two values (frequency in hertz and duration in milliseconds) to change the sound of the beep. You can play a beep sound on its own or line up several lines to produce more complex sounds or even little tunes, which can be made to play in the background.

In one of my own little games, I use the beep function when the player gets killed.

```
[console]::beep(440, 200)
[console]::beep(340, 200)
[console]::beep(240, 200)
[console]::beep(149, 200)
```

You can even introduce pauses to create more interesting tunes using the Start-Sleep cmdlet. Pass this cmdlet a number, and the script will pause for that many milliseconds:

```
Start-Sleep -m 300
```

Online there are several great tunes made using beep; go and Google "star wars powershell beep." On there, you can download theme tunes for Star Wars, Super Mario, and Mission Impossible!

Have a go at making your own tunes to use in scripts and games of your own.

© Ian Waters 2021
I. Waters, *PowerShell for Beginners*, https://doi.org/10.1007/978-1-4842-7064-6_18

Playing wav Files

If you want to play proper music files or recorded audio or just premade sound effects, you can use the SoundPlayer class to play wav files. Using the SoundPlayer class, we simply need to instantiate an object from the class, specify the location of the wav file, and play the file using the Play method. Once we are finished with the object, simply call the Dispose method to clean up the used memory.

```
$sound = New-Object System.Media.SoundPlayer

$sound.SoundLocation = "C:\scripts\sound.wav"

$sound.Play()

$sound.Dispose()
```

Being able to play back proper sound files opens up a world of possibilities for writing your own fun little scripts.

Making PowerShell Speak

Using .Net classes, we can even make a PowerShell script talk! This can be a lot of fun and great for developing scripts for people with poor eyesight, for young children, or, like this whole book, just for the fun of it. If you think robots are going to take over the world, well, you may be right. Let's hear what PowerShell sounds like.

First, we use the Add-Type cmdlet to make the .Net speech classes available to our PowerShell session. We then create an object from the SpeechSynthesizer class, which handles converting a string of text into audible speech.

```
#Define .Net Class to use in session
Add-Type -AssemblyName System.speech

#Instanciate an object from the SpeechSynthesizer class
$speak = New-Object System.Speech.Synthesis.SpeechSynthesizer
```

```
#Speak the text from the speakers
$speak.Speak("Would you like to play a game?")

#Clean up used memory
$speak.Dispose()
```

Pretty cool, right?!

Using a method from the SpeechSynthesizer class, we can also set the output to go to a local wav file rather than playing it out via the speakers. You may want to do this to use the sound file in another project or to avoid converting the text on the fly in the script. Either way it's a pretty useful method to take advantage of.

```
#Define .Net Class to use in session
Add-Type -AssemblyName System.speech

#Instanciate an object from the SpeechSynthesizer class
$speak = New-Object System.Speech.Synthesis.SpeechSynthesizer

#Change the output to a local wav file
$speak.SetOutputToWaveFile("C:\scripts\sound.wav")

#Speak the text to the wav file
$speak.Speak("Would you like to play a game?")

#Clean up used memory
$speak.Dispose()
```

Once you run the script, it should produce a wav sound file in the Scripts folder as shown in Figure 18-1. Play the sound file to hear the text-to-speech audio.

Figure 18-1. *Add a sound file to the c:\Scripts project folder*

Conclusion

Well, that was fun, and now you know how to make basic beep sounds, play wav sound files, and even make PowerShell talk! Use these lessons to produce more interactive and immersive scripts of your own.

Game Engine

If you've been with me from the beginning of this book, then a quick congratulations to you! I love it when someone wants to learn something new, picks up a book, and cracks on with it. Now you have learned a huge chunk of the basics, and now we can have a little more fun and start to build some scripts into a proper functional game. Now this isn't what PowerShell is meant for, and it's not even that great at it, but the point is we can and it's fun and helps us learn to code. So in this chapter, I'm going to walk you through one way you can build out a game using all of the code you have learned so far. First, we need to create a very basic game engine. This is essentially code that makes the game work, loads the title screen, loads the level graphics, loads in players in the game, and sets up how the player can move the character around the screen and how the player gets points and completes levels.

This game engine is the basis for a few of my own games, and one of my first and most played is Power Invaders, my own little PowerShell version of the classic Space Invaders! The basic code structure can be expanded further to create a top-down game such as Gauntlet and Pac Man or even a side-scrolling platform game. The options are limitless and up to your own imagination and creativity.

I've included the full source code of Power Invaders in the code bundle: Chapter 19\ PowerInvaders\. Use this chapter to understand how I've built out the game engine and play around with the code to make your own modifications.

Game Engine Layout

Ok, so a game engine needs to do quite a few small tasks, so each task can generally be regarded as a function of its own or be combined into a class with several methods and properties. Let's take a quick look at a few of the main tasks so you know what sort of things we will be talking about.

© Ian Waters 2021
I. Waters, *PowerShell for Beginners*, https://doi.org/10.1007/978-1-4842-7064-6_19

The Setup Phase

In the setup phase, the game engine will need to set the display and load configuration files, title screens, and objects used in the game, and we will do this in the following order:

1.   Set up the display to the required size.

2.   Load a game configuration file.

3.   Load a title screen from a text file.

4.   Load each object and character from text files.

The Title Screen

When the game engine starts, one of the first things the player will see is the title screen. We will create our title screen and game over screen using basic text files using ASCII art and use our old friend Get-Content to read those files into an array of strings we can write out to the console. We've not touched on ASCII art, but it's basically the art of drawing pictures using the alphabet, numbers, and special characters. We will explore this in greater detail in the next chapter, but since this is a text-based game, we need to build out the screens and objects using only text characters.

•   Display the title screen until the player presses a key to play.

The Game Loop

Once the player has entered the game from the title screen, we need to enter the main game loop, which keeps repeating until the player dies or completes the game. The steps are broken down in the following, and we should be able to set up separate functions for each of these steps to keep the code well organized:

1.   Draw the level background to the display.

2.   Draw the game objects to the screen.

3.   Detect if any objects hit each other.

4.   Run each object's "behavior script."

5.   Detect key presses from the player and move the character on the screen.

The Game Over Screen

The final step in the process is to display the game over screen in the same way we did displaying the title screen. We will draw it out in a text file and read the content using Get-Content and write it out to the console.

- Draw the game over screen and wait for the player to press a key and then loop back to the title screen.

Ok, now let's take a look at each of these sections in more detail and at the code and start building!

The Setup Phase

Set Up the Display to the Required Size

In the setup phase of our script, we need to set the display to a suitable gaming size. Luckily we created a handy little function back in Chapter 9. We can reuse that in the engine to set the width, height, and window title text:

```
function Setup-Display([string]$title, [int]$width, [int]$height) {
    $psHost = get-host
    $window = $psHost.ui.rawui
    $newsize = $window.WindowSize
    $newsize.Height = $height
    $newsize.Width = $width
    $window.WindowSize = $newsize
    $window.WindowTitle = $title
}
```

A good size for a game console is around 110 characters wide and 56 lines high. We can make it easy to reference the display size by using a couple of global variables. As learned from Chapter 3, global variables have a wider scope than normal variables in that they can be accessed in more places throughout your code. This is particularly important since we will need to access many of the main game variables from different classes and scripts, which will run independently of the main script:

```
$global:displayWidth = 110
$global:displayHeight = 56
```

So at the start of our code, we can use the following to set up the display:

```
#Clear screen
Clear-Host

#Set powershell console window to required size
Setup-Display $global:gameName $global:displayWidth $global:displayHeight
```

Load a Game Configuration File

A generic game engine can be configured to run lots of different games simply by editing a configuration file. The config file defines where the title, game over, end of game, and game complete screens are. It also states the number of levels in the game and describes how each level should work.

In my game engine, the game config file is simply a text file. At the top of the file, each of the game screens is defined. Each line will start with the name of the thing being set up, so the first line lists TITLESCREEN and then a colon followed by the name of the file that contains the title screen graphics.

Next is GAMEOVERSCREEN and then a colon followed by the name of the file that contains the game over screen graphics and so on.

Each level starts with a STARTLEVEL: tag and ends with an ENDLEVEL: tag. Everything between these tags defines what the level is called, what file is called that includes the level background graphics, and also a SPAWN: tag, which defines an object in the game.

SPAWN tags are used to add an object to the level. The tag includes the object configuration filename followed by three numbers. The first is a timer value; this tells the engine when the character should be spawned into the level. The last two numbers are X and Y location values defining where to place the object within the level.

The following is an example game config file from my own Power Invaders game. It contains two levels, a player character, an enemy character, and a block object, an object that can't be killed or moved. I use these to create shielded areas the player can hide behind:

```
TITLESCREEN:TITLESCREEN.TXT
GAMEOVERSCREEN:GAMEOVERSCREEN.TXT
ENDGAMESCREEN:QUITSCREEN.TXT
GAMECOMPLETESCREEN:COMPLETESCREEN.TXT
```

```
STARTLEVEL:
NAME:LEVEL1
BACKGROUND:LEVEL1.TXT
SPAWN:PLAYER1.TXT:0:10:50
SPAWN:HIDEBLOCK.TXT:0:11:44
SPAWN:HIDEBLOCK.TXT:0:38:44
SPAWN:HIDEBLOCK.TXT:0:65:44
SPAWN:HIDEBLOCK.TXT:0:92:44
SPAWN:ENEMY1.TXT:0:20:5
SPAWN:ENEMY1.TXT:0:35:5
SPAWN:ENEMY1.TXT:0:50:5
ENDLEVEL:
STARTLEVEL:
NAME:LEVEL2
BACKGROUND:LEVEL1.TXT
SPAWN:PLAYER1.TXT:0:10:50
SPAWN:HIDEBLOCK.TXT:0:11:44
SPAWN:HIDEBLOCK.TXT:0:38:44
SPAWN:HIDEBLOCK.TXT:0:65:44
SPAWN:HIDEBLOCK.TXT:0:92:44
SPAWN:ENEMY1.TXT:0:20:5
SPAWN:ENEMY1.TXT:0:35:5
SPAWN:ENEMY1.TXT:0:50:5
SPAWN:ENEMY1.TXT:0:65:5
ENDLEVEL:
```

Now that we have a config file for the game, we need to use everything we have learned from Chapters 6 and 17 to build a function that can read this file and assign the correct values to our main gaming variables and start adding objects to the levels.

For this task, I've created a Load-GameConfig function in the main game script. The first cmdlet in the function is called to read the content of the config file into an array. Since we know the layout of the config file, we know exactly what the first four variables are and in which order they are listed, so we can simply move these values into the global variables for the title, game over, end of game, and game complete screens. The only issue is that we need to remove the tag name and the colon because the value we want is the part after the colon.

To do this, we can use the Split method available to string object types. Split will divide up a string based on a value you pass into it, and it will return an array of text values split up by the character you passed it. So if we pass it a colon, it will return an array containing two values, "TITLESCREEN" and "TITLESCREEN.TXT." Since we only want the actual value, we can reference the second entry in the array and feed the result directly into the global variable.

Remember the second entry in an array is referenced with a 1 since the first entry in an array is at position 0.

Spend some time examining this code because it can look very complicated, but really it's not. It's simply using a for loop to look at every line in the config file and look for tags such as STARTLEVEL, ENDLEVEL, and SPAWN. Then depending on what tags it finds, it enters the correct place in the if else statement and continues to read lines capturing the required variable values into a Levels class. I've not included the full code here as it's quite long but included the just the Load-GameConfig function for you to review first. Locate the PowerInvaders.ps1 script in the Chapter 19 code bundle to explorer the compete script:

```
$global:titleScreen = $lines[0].Split(':')[1]
function Load-GameConfig($gameConfig) {
    #Read file content into lines
    $lines = Get-Content $gameConfig
    $global:titleScreen = $lines[0].Split(':')[1]
    $global:gameOverScreen = $lines[1].Split(':')[1]
    $global:endGameScreen = $lines[2].Split(':')[1]
    $global:gameCompleteScreen = $lines[3].Split(':')[1]
    $global:levels = New-Object System.Collections.ArrayList
    $global:gameLevelCount = 0

    for ($i = 0; $i -lt $lines.Length; $i++) {
        if ($lines[$i] -eq "STARTLEVEL:") {
            $global:levels += New-Object Level
            $levelObjectCount = 0
            $i++
            while ($lines[$i] -ne "ENDLEVEL:") {
```

```
        if ($lines[$i].StartsWith("NAME:",
        "CurrentCultureIgnoreCase")) {
            $global:levels[$global:gameLevelCount].name =
            $lines[$i].Split(':')[1]
        }
        elseif ($lines[$i].StartsWith("BACKGROUND:",
        "CurrentCultureIgnoreCase")) {
            $global:levels[$global:gameLevelCount].background =
            $lines[$i].Split(':')[1]
        }
        elseif ($lines[$i].StartsWith("SPAWN:",
        "CurrentCultureIgnoreCase")) {
            $index = $global:levels[$global:gameLevelCount].
            objects.Add((New-Object GameObject))
            $global:levels[$global:gameLevelCount].objects
            [$levelObjectCount].LoadObject($lines[$i].Split(':')[1])
            $global:levels[$global:gameLevelCount].objects
            [$levelObjectCount].xPosition = $lines[$i].Split(':')[3]
            $global:levels[$global:gameLevelCount].objects
            [$levelObjectCount].yPosition = $lines[$i].Split(':')[4]

            $levelObjectCount++
        }

        $i++
    }
    $global:gameLevelCount++
    }
  }
}
```

Load a Title Screen from a Text File

In the game, a title screen or level background will just be text-based graphics stored as an array of string objects. When we need to display a title screen or level background, we simply draw each of these strings to the console window using a Write-Host cmdlet.

Using code learned from Chapter 17, we know there is a handy cmdlet Get-Content that can do exactly what we need. It reads each line from a text file and returns an array of string objects. Brilliant! We can wrap this little cmdlet into a function so that we can use it for loading any screen or level background we need by passing in the filename:

```
function Load-Level([string]$file) {
    return Get-Content $file
}
```

By creating a nice title screen using a text file, which is 111 characters wide and 55 lines long, we can use the Load-Level function to read the contents and then call Write-Host to display that text to the screen and display a nice screen to the player as shown in Figure in 19-1.

Figure 19-1. *Power Invaders title screen – PowerShell wasn't meant for this, but it looks awesome:)*

Load Each Object and Character from Text Files

Just like we have used a configuration file for the game defining the levels and objects, we can use the same technique for the objects themselves. Objects in a level can be anything that sits within the level such as an enemy character, bomb, rocket, special power-up, doorway, or just scenery. Objects have special abilities because in the game engine, we will set up collision detection code so that the player and none of the other objects in the level can bump into each other.

Just like with the game config file, the object config files start with a few basic tags defining the object's name, speed, and height and width of the object's graphics.

Under basic information, there is a FRAMES tag, which defines the number of animation frames that will get displayed when the object moves followed by the object's graphics. In the following example, you can see that there is one frame and some # symbols, which make up how the object will look on the screen, which is exactly 6 characters high and 9 characters wide.

At the end of the config file, we have two tags, MOVESCRIPTSTART: and MOVESCRIPTEND:. These are used to define the behavior of the object. Within these two tags, we can write standard PowerShell code that will get called and run between each loop/frame of the game.

You might be wondering why I have included code in the object configuration file rather than coding it directly into a script file? Well, I could have; but in my design, I wanted to have a class that represented all types of objects. Since players, other characters, and in-game objects all have the same basic components, I wanted to use a single class to represent them all. I could have added movement code for each of the different types of objects into the class, but I wanted to leave it as generic as possible, so I decided to add the movement scripts to the object configuration files. That way, if I ever wanted to add a new object or enemy character, I just needed to create a new object configuration file.

This is how many real-world game engines work, and in-game objects often have their own scripting files so the movement and behavior is not hard coded into the engine itself.

If you wanted to do it the other way, you could. You could create a class for each type of object that inherits from the game object class. It's like taking the basics and adding to it or changing parts of it to create a class that does something more specific. We are not covering class inheritance in this book, but it's definitely something for you to advance on to later in further studies.

Ok, let's take a look at what a game object configuration file looks like:

```
NAME:ENEMY
SPEED:5
HEIGHT:6
WIDTH:9
FRAMES:1
   ###
 #######
## # # ##
##     ##
   ###
  #   #
MOVESCRIPTSTART:
$leftBoundry = 4
$rightBoundry = 96

if($this.xPosition -le $leftBoundry)
{
      if($this.sTimer -ge $this.speed)
      {
            $this.yPosition = $this.yPosition + 7
            $this.direction = "right"
      }
}
elseif($this.xPosition -ge $rightBoundry)
{
      if($this.sTimer -ge $this.speed)
      {
            $this.yPosition = $this.yPosition + 7
            $this.direction = "left"
      }
}

if($this.direction -eq "right")
{
      if($this.sTimer -ge $this.speed)
```

```
        {
                $this.xPosition++
                $this.sTimer = 0
        }
}
else
{
        if($this.sTimer -ge $this.speed)
        {
                $this.xPosition--
                $this.sTimer = 0
        }
}

if($this.yPosition -ge 40)
{
        $this.yPosition = 5
}

#Randomly drop a bomb
$random = Get-Random -Minimum 1 -Maximum 1000
if($random -ge 990)
{
        $bomb = New-Object GameObject
        $bomb.LoadObject("Bomb.txt")
        $bomb.xPosition = $this.xPosition + 4
        $bomb.yPosition = $this.yPosition + 6
        $global:levels[$global:currentLevel].objects.Add($bomb)
}

$this.sTimer++

MOVESCRIPTEND:
```

As we have seen before in the Load-Level function where tags are used to locate and read information back into variables, we do the same here – storing what the object looks like, how big it is, and how it moves in the game by using PowerShell code within the MOVESCRIPTSTART and MOVESCRIPTEND tags.

Solving the Screen Flicker Problem

At this point, I need to explain an issue that plagues all games especially ones written in PowerShell because, as I've said before, it's not designed for this sort of thing, but it is a common problem for games old and new. It's that to build a frame in the game, we need to draw the background and move the cursor around to draw each of the objects and game characters and show a high score and other information. This whizzing around the screen causes the display to flicker and look nasty. You can see the cursor moving around drawing text to the console, and it's just not fast enough. In modern computer games, this is also a problem; and to solve it, they use a technique called double buffering.

This technique basically involves drawing everything you need for a frame into memory before shooting that memory to the screen. It's much quicker to draw lines of the screen in order one by one than jumping around the screen. This buffering results in a much nicer and mostly flicker-free game.

In our game engine, we will use this technique by "drawing" all of the content for the screen to an array of strings first; then once everything has been drawn into the array, we can very quickly dump the whole array to the console screen in one go. That also means we don't have to move the console cursor; we just need to edit the text within the strings, which will also be much faster.

We will do that by defining a screen buffer, and we will draw everything to that first and then in one go write it out to the console reducing the flickering, and it stops the cursor jumping all over the screen:

```
[Array]$global:screenBuffer = @()
```

When we want that screen buffer displayed to the console, we can call the following function:

```
function Draw-Buffer()
{
    for($i = 0;$i -lt $global:screenBuffer.Count;$i++)
    {
        $global:screenBuffer[$i]
    }
}
```

The Game Loop

Once the game configuration file has been loaded and all of the objects and game screens have been loaded, the engine displays the title screen and waits for the player to press a key. Once a key is pressed, the main game loop kicks in. The game loop is where the magic happens and all of the code comes together to create a functional game.

The game loop has the following jobs:

- Draw the level background to the screen buffer.

- Draw each of the level objects to the screen buffer.

- Detect player input and move the player's character.

- Run the game logic for each of the level's objects.

- Check to see if any objects collide and if they do act accordingly.

- Detect if the player has completed the level.

- Detect if the player has died and end the current game.

The following is the main game loop from our little game engine. You can see it first sets up the display and then enters a while loop, which continues to run while the player does not press the Q key during the title screen.

Next, a few global variables are initialized; then the game config file and all of the main screens and objects are loaded.

Next, the title screen is loaded and the screen buffer cleared and drawn to display the title screen graphics to the console.

The next level in the game is initialized; then the main game loop is entered. From here the game engine will update the screen, run the behavior code for each object, detect player key presses, and move the player's character along with detecting collisions.

The loop continues until either the player dies or the player wins the level. If the player dies, then the game over screen is shown, and the $global:gameLoopRunning variable gets set to false. The game then resets and displays the title screen again. If the player wins the game, the next level is loaded and the game loop continues again.

Study the following code and try and follow it round the various loops to get to grips with how it works:

```
#Start Running Program Commands

#Clear screen
Clear-Host

#Set powershell console window to required size
Setup-Display $global:gameName global:displayWidth $global:displayHeight

while (!$global:exitGame) {
    #Clear screen and initialise global variables
    cls
    $global:currentLevel = -1
    $global:gameLoopRunning = $True
    $global:backgroundBuffer = @()
    $global:screenBuffer = @()
    Load-GameConfig("GameConfig.txt")

    #Display title screen and wait for player to confirm start
    $global:backgroundBuffer = Load-Level "TitleScreen.txt"
    Clear-ScreenBuffer
    Draw-ScreenBuffer

    #Wait for user to press any key to being the game
    $continue = $host.UI.RawUI.ReadKey("NoEcho,IncludeKeyDown")

    Load-NextLevel

    while ($global:gameLoopRunning) {
        #Draw the screen objects to the buffer
        #Then draw the buffer to the console window
        Draw-ScreenBuffer

        #Check for player input and move character
        #Also check for object collisions
        Run-GameLogic
```

```
    #See if player got killed and restart game
    if ($global:levels[$global:currentLevel].objects[0].IsDead()) {
        Player-Dead
    }

    Remove-DeadObjects

    #Check to see if player has won the level
    if (Detect-LevelWin) {
        #level up
        Load-NextLevel

        #Check if the player and won the whole game
        Detect-GameWin
    }
  }
}

#Display quit screen
$global:backgroundBuffer = Load-Level "QuitScreen.txt"
Clear-ScreenBuffer
Draw-ScreenBuffer

#Display the Quit screen for a few seconds before finishing
Start-Sleep -s 7

#Clear screen
Clear-Host
```

Now you can put it all together and have a game of Power Invaders!

Review the full code listing in the Chapter 19 code bundle and run PowerInvaders. ps1 and have a few games yourself. If all is working correctly, you should see it run as shown in Figure 19-2.

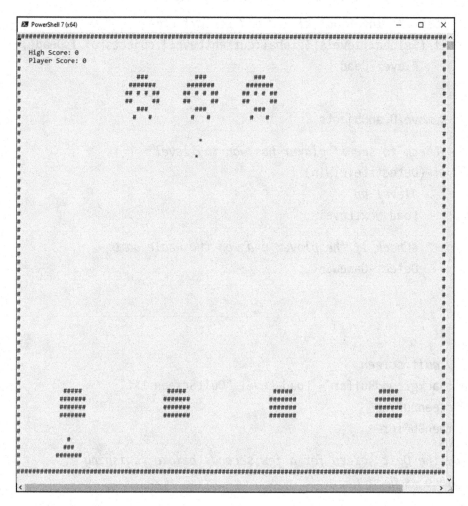

Figure 19-2. *Screenshot from level 1 of Power Invaders*

Conclusion

Wow, that was quite a chapter! If you have followed through the chapter and studied the code in detail, then you are now equipped to write your own fully fledged old-school PowerShell games! You have truly come a long way since you started this book. From humble beginnings, you are becoming truly proficient in PowerShell and able to read, understand, and write complex PowerShell scripts. Good job!

Creating Game Artwork

Creating ASCII artwork is actually kinda fun. Designing cool-looking levels, game objects, and title screens using plaintext can be a challenge. I've dedicated a whole chapter to give you a few tips and to show you a few bits of artwork from my own game, Power Invaders.

Building a Title Screen

When you build a title screen, it helps to put # or another character around the border of the gaming area. This helps you see the size and positioning when the screen will be displayed into the PowerShell console window. For the game Power Invaders, I use a console window of 110 characters wide and 56 characters high:

```
$global:displayWidth = 110
$global:displayHeight = 56
```

This means your first line in the title screen will be 110 characters and for the height you create 56 lines, starting each with your chosen border character. We have to use one less line than our console window; otherwise, when the last line is drawn to the screen, the cursor goes to the next line and pushes the first line off the window, and this creates a nasty flickering screen, so just remember that when building your own levels and in-game screens.

Figure 20-1 is the title screen from Power Invaders, and you can see I used a border to define the window area and used a mixture of text and ASCII art to include characters and the game title.

© Ian Waters 2021
I. Waters, *PowerShell for Beginners*, https://doi.org/10.1007/978-1-4842-7064-6_20

Figure 20-1. *Power Invaders title screen design in a text file*

For this one, I made the ASCII artwork manually just using the # symbol. It's simple but quite effective and looks great when displayed in a PowerShell console window.

ASCII Art Generators

There are a number of online services that can take some text or an image and convert it into awesome ASCII art automatically for you. You can swipe the output and use it in your scripts and games. It's amazing how good some pictures and words look when run through an ASCII generator, and I use them all the time when creating graphics for personal projects.

ASCII Text

Here is a quick list of generators that I have used to develop my own scripts and game artwork, but there are lots of others you can use and experiment with:

```
https://asciiartgen.now.sh
www.ascii-art-generator.org/
www.network-science.de/ascii/
```

ASCII-Art-Generator.org allows you to enter some text and define if the output is colored or black text and allows you to define the width of each line. Defining the width is a really nice feature because our game windows are of a fixed width, so this makes it easy to keep the artwork within the limits of our console window. Here Figure 20-2 shows how you can define the size of the image and pass in some text to generate it as ASCII art in the required size.

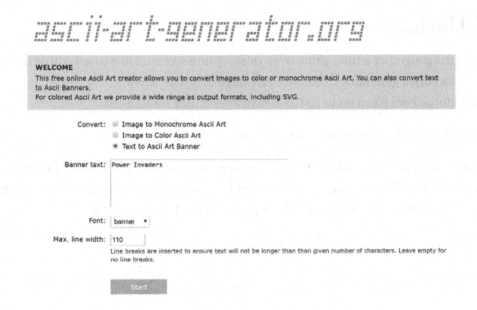

Figure 20-2. *ASCII-Art-Generator website. Enter the text you want to convert to ASCII art and click start*

Simply click Start and the output is generated. Simply copy and paste the ASCII artwork into your script, and away you go as shown in Figure 20-3.

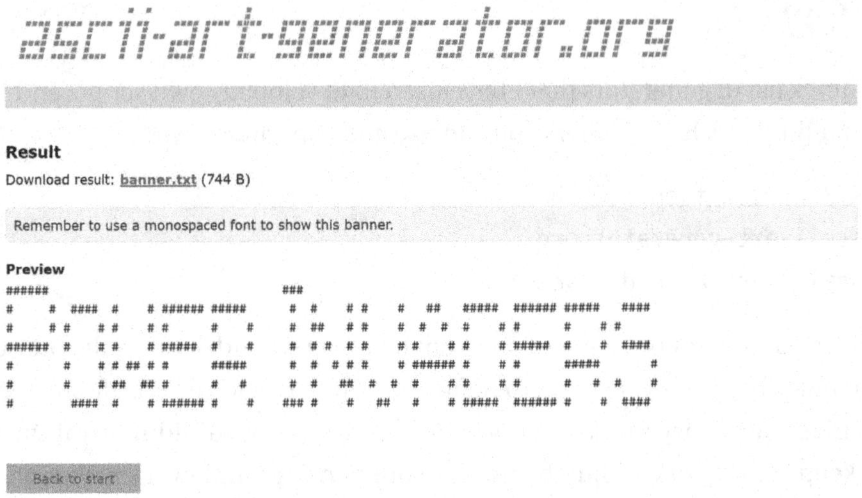

Figure 20-3. *ASCII-Art-Generator website*

ASCII Images

When putting together a title, game over, or story line screen, I like to get a little more creative and use a generator to convert an image to ASCII artwork.

Sporkforge.com has a great ASCII artwork generator for images:

```
http://sporkforge.com/imaging/ascii.php
```

Simply upload your image and it will generate awesome ASCII for you. I used this one in the Dragon Slayer script we worked on in this book. In Figure 20-4, you can see a button to upload a jpeg image, and this is great fun to play around with.

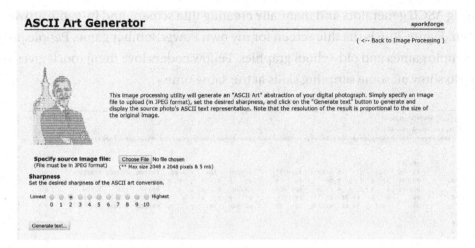

Figure 20-4. *Sporkforge.com website*

I used the output as the basic starting point and added some text. These generators make the process a whole lot quicker than trying to manually design your own images from scratch. Figure 20-5 shows the output of a dragon image I uploaded, and it looks awesome.

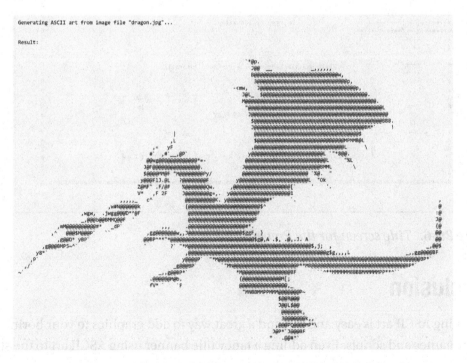

Figure 20-5. *Generating ASCII art for the Dragon Slayer game*

Using ASCII generators and manually creating title screens and in-game artwork is great fun. Figure 20-6 is the title screen for my own PowerBomber game. People just love these simple games and old-school graphics. Fellow coders love them too. It gives you a chance to show off some scripting skills at the same time.

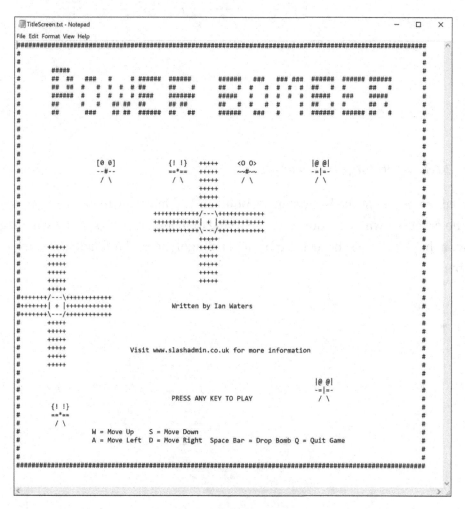

Figure 20-6. *Title screen for the PowerBomber game*

Conclusion

Generating ASCII art is easy and fun and a great way to add graphics to your boring-looking games and scripts. Even adding a fancy title banner using ASCII art to the start of your scripts will set you apart from other PowerShell programmers out there.

PowerBomber

PowerBomber is a fun little game I wrote while experimenting with pathfinding algorithms using PowerShell. Testing out some code, I ended up actually writing a Bomberman-type game using the game engine code we've been studying in this book. I'm going to walk you through each part of the code that makes up the game and briefly go over the algorithm used, which allows the characters to move around the screen on their own. It's pretty cool stuff, and if you follow along with it, you will become even more proficient in using PowerShell, which is our ultimate goal.

Rather than list the individual snippets of code in this chapter, I have included the full game code and supported files in the Chapter 21 code bundle for you to explore at your leisure.

Let's get started.

Game Design

This game is going to build on the game engine code shown in Chapter 19. Since we already have the engine code and we know how to implement title and game over screens, build levels, and add objects and players to the levels, this should be fairly straightforward. Let's first take a look again at the basic flow of the game code. Then we will look more closely again at the code itself and see how we can make the enemy characters more intelligent and make them move around the screen on their own and even avoid other objects in the level.

Code Flow

It's often helpful to break out a pen and paper and plan the flow of code in scripts you write, especially if you are writing a large complicated script like this one. Doing this also helps you start to work on the different functions you will need to write to build the script.

© Ian Waters 2021
I. Waters, *PowerShell for Beginners*, https://doi.org/10.1007/978-1-4842-7064-6_21

In the following diagram, you can see that the script starts up and first loads the game configuration file. This file defines all of the screens, levels, and objects in each level. Next, the title screen loads up and waits for the player to press a key to continue. The next level including the background and all objects in the level get loaded. Then the main game loop starts.

At the start of the game loop, the player's movements are managed. Then each object in the level has its own behavior code run. This lets all of the enemy players, bullets, and bombs move around or explode.

Next, the code detects if the player died; and if they did, the game over screen is displayed and the script ends. If the player is still alive, the script detects if the player has won the level. If they have, the next level is loaded and the game loop continues. If they haven't won, the script finally checks if the player has won the full game. If they have, the game complete screen is displayed and then the script ends. If they haven't won the game yet, the game loops repeats again.

The loop continues until the player dies or the player completes the game.

Figure 21-1 shows the flow of the code graphically, and I often like to do this when designing large and complicated scripts. It helps to break down code into manageable sections.

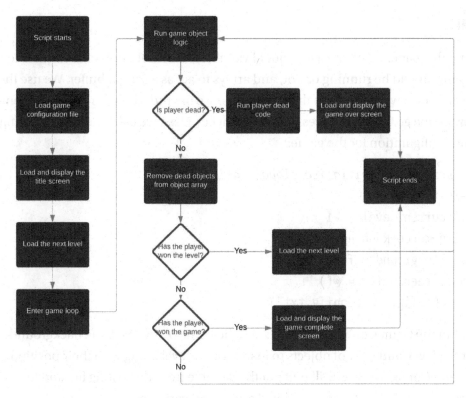

Figure 21-1. *PowerBomber game engine code flow*

Working on this flow diagram highlights a few sections of code we will need to work on. Since the game engine code handles most of these elements, most of the work will be in writing the logic required to make the enemy players and objects work in the game. That's the beauty of reusable code. Other projects like this become easier because we've done most of the hard work before.

Keep your code reusable and organized on your computer as you write scripts. This will make future projects much quicker and easier to work on.

Let's recap a few bits within the game engine we reviewed in Chapter 19 and go over each of the phases within the script.

Setup

To set up the game, we create a few global variables, the level number, a variable to know if the game should be running or not, and arrays to act as a screen buffer. We use the screen buffers to write text onto them first; then we fire the whole screen to the console window in one go, which reduces the screen flicker. Next, we call Load-GameConfig to load the configuration for the game:

```
#Clear screen and initialise global variables
Clear-Host
$global:currentLevel = -1
$global:gameLoopRunning = $True
$global:backgroundBuffer = @()
$global:screenBuffer = @()
Load-GameConfig("GameConfig.txt")
```

Within the GameConfig.txt file, we store the name of the level, the background file to use for the level, and a list of objects to load into the level along with their positions. The Load-GameConfig function will pull out the variable from this config file and load each of the screens and objects into the global arrays and variables.

Here is part of the config file from PowerBomber. Review it to understand how the information is structured. Each item starts with the item type, and then the value of that type comes after the colon. The code loops through each line and loads the items into global variables. First, the game screens get loaded, title screen, game over screen, and so on, into global variables. Then each level and level objects get loaded into the Levels class object and ultimately into an object array to be used during the game:

```
TITLESCREEN:TITLESCREEN.TXT
GAMEOVERSCREEN:GAMEOVERSCREEN.TXT
ENDGAMESCREEN:QUITSCREEN.TXT
GAMECOMPLETESCREEN:COMPLETESCREEN.TXT

STARTLEVEL:
NAME:LEVEL1
BACKGROUND:LEVEL1.TXT
SPAWN:PLAYER1.TXT:0:1:5
SPAWN:PORTAL.TXT:0:91:41
SPAWN:ENEMY1.TXT:0:101:47
```

```
SPAWN:BLOCK.TXT:0:51:23
SPAWN:BLOCK.TXT:0:56:20
SPAWN:BLOCK.TXT:0:61:17
SPAWN:BLOCK.TXT:0:46:20
SPAWN:BLOCK.TXT:0:41:17
SPAWN:BLOCK.TXT:0:46:26
SPAWN:BLOCK.TXT:0:41:29
SPAWN:BLOCK.TXT:0:56:26
SPAWN:BLOCK.TXT:0:61:29
SPAWN:BLOCK2.TXT:0:51:20
SPAWN:BLOCK2.TXT:0:51:26
SPAWN:BLOCK2.TXT:0:46:23
SPAWN:BLOCK2.TXT:0:56:23
ENDLEVEL:

STARTLEVEL:
NAME:LEVEL2
BACKGROUND:LEVEL1.TXT
SPAWN:PLAYER1.TXT:0:1:5
SPAWN:ENEMY1.TXT:0:101:47
SPAWN:PORTAL.TXT:0:91:11
SPAWN:BLOCK.TXT:0:11:5
SPAWN:BLOCK.TXT:0:11:8
SPAWN:BLOCK.TXT:0:11:11
SPAWN:BLOCK.TXT:0:11:14
SPAWN:BLOCK.TXT:0:11:17
SPAWN:BLOCK.TXT:0:11:20
SPAWN:BLOCK.TXT:0:16:20
SPAWN:BLOCK.TXT:0:21:20
SPAWN:BLOCK.TXT:0:26:20
SPAWN:BLOCK.TXT:0:31:20
SPAWN:BLOCK.TXT:0:36:20
SPAWN:BLOCK.TXT:0:41:20
SPAWN:BLOCK.TXT:0:46:20
SPAWN:BLOCK.TXT:0:51:20
SPAWN:BLOCK.TXT:0:51:23
```

```
SPAWN:BLOCK2.TXT:0:51:26
SPAWN:BLOCK.TXT:0:51:29
SPAWN:BLOCK2.TXT:0:51:32
SPAWN:BLOCK.TXT:0:51:35
SPAWN:BLOCK2.TXT:0:51:38
SPAWN:BLOCK.TXT:0:51:41
SPAWN:BLOCK2.TXT:0:51:44
SPAWN:BLOCK.TXT:0:51:47
ENDLEVEL:
```

Title Screen

The title screen is put together in Notepad or your favorite text editor. You can use ASCII art or an ASCII generator to help build out nice-looking graphics. Then we can use the Load-Level function to read the title screen file into the global backgroundBuffer array. We can then push the background buffer to the screen by calling Draw-BackgroundToScreenBuffer and then call Draw-Buffer. We then wait for the player to press a key to start the game. Finally, we call Load-NextLevel to set up all of the objects within level 1 ready for the main game loop to start:

```
#Display title screen and wait for player to confirm start
$global:backgroundBuffer = Load-Level "TitleScreen.txt"
Clear-ScreenBuffer
Move-Cursor 0 0
Draw-BackgroundtoScreenBuffer
Draw-Buffer

#Wait for user to press any key
$Host.UI.RawUI.FlushInputBuffer()
$continue = $host.UI.RawUI.ReadKey("NoEcho,IncludeKeyDown")

#Increase the level number and load the levels background image (array)
into the global backgroundbuffer array
Load-NextLevel
```

Here in Figure 21-2 is the title screen for PowerBomber saved as a TitleScreen.txt file. We use the Load-Level function to read the content of the file and store it into the background buffer array to display it to the screen when the game starts.

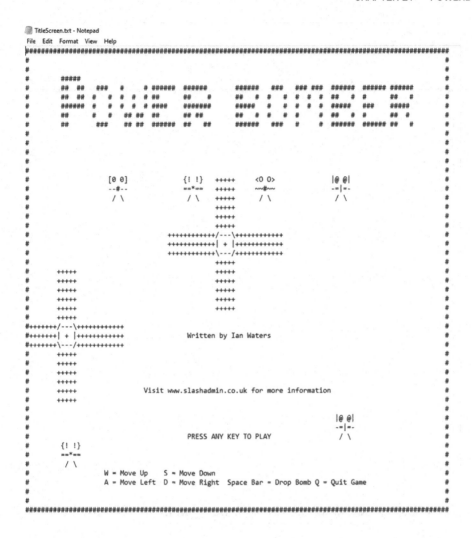

Figure 21-2. *PowerBomber game title screen*

Levels

PowerBomber uses the same level background for each level, and again it's designed and saved into a text file, and the Load-Level function is used to read the contents of the file and return an array of strings.

PowerBomber just uses one level background graphics text file as shown in Figure 21-3. I use this for all of the levels and simply change the levels by adding different objects to each one.

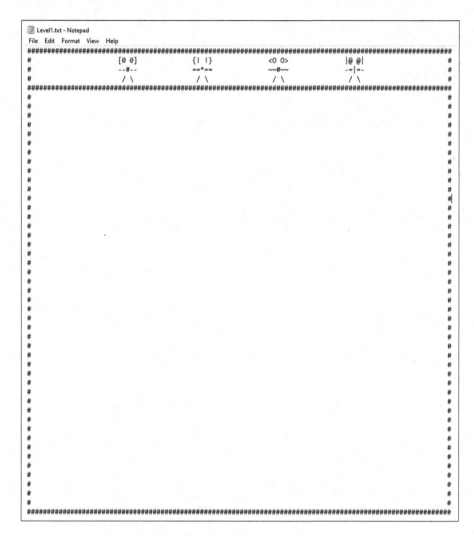

Figure 21-3. *PowerBomber level background file*

As you've seen previously, each level gets saved in the GameConfig.txt file as a new STARTLEVEL: ENDLEVEL: pair. Everything between those tags defines what objects are to be used in the game, the level name, and the background image to use in the level. After that the SPAWN tag is used to define what objects are loaded into the level during gameplay starting with the player's character.

Each SPAWN tag is broken down into the object configuration filename, followed by the time in seconds to appear in the level and the X and Y positions:

```
STARTLEVEL:
NAME:LEVEL1
BACKGROUND:LEVEL1.TXT
SPAWN:PLAYER1.TXT:0:1:5
SPAWN:PORTAL.TXT:0:91:41
SPAWN:ENEMY1.TXT:0:101:47
SPAWN:BLOCK.TXT:0:51:23
SPAWN:BLOCK.TXT:0:56:20
SPAWN:BLOCK.TXT:0:61:17
SPAWN:BLOCK.TXT:0:46:20
SPAWN:BLOCK.TXT:0:41:17
SPAWN:BLOCK.TXT:0:46:26
SPAWN:BLOCK.TXT:0:41:29
SPAWN:BLOCK.TXT:0:56:26
SPAWN:BLOCK.TXT:0:61:29
SPAWN:BLOCK2.TXT:0:51:20
SPAWN:BLOCK2.TXT:0:51:26
SPAWN:BLOCK2.TXT:0:46:23
SPAWN:BLOCK2.TXT:0:56:23
ENDLEVEL:
```

The object configuration files work in much the same way, defining what the character looks like and what code to run at each iteration around the game loop. We will take a look at how the game object configuration file works shortly, but first let's fire up a couple of levels from PowerBomber and take a look! Figure 21-4 shows level 1 of PowerBomber; it looks pretty impressive even if I do say so myself! I'm old-school and love the classic retro look. When you play with the code, experiment with the game configuration file and modify the levels to build some of your own.

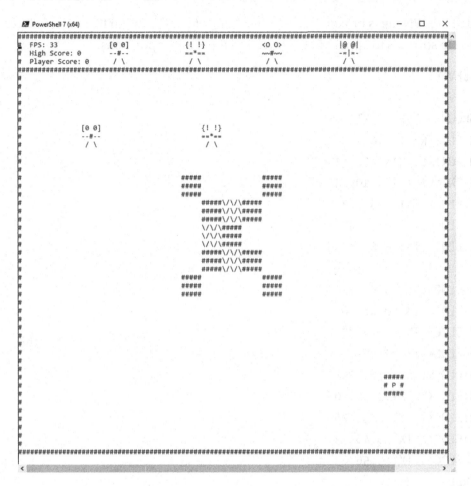

Figure 21-4. *PowerBomber level 1*

In Figure 21-5, you can see the explodable block, which can be killed off by exploding a bomb next to it, and a portal block, which when touched triggers the next level sequence.

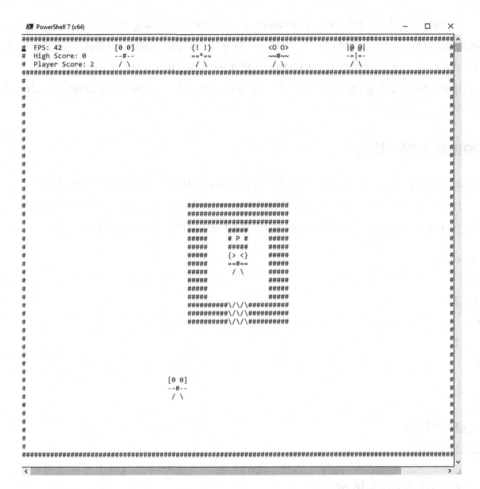

Figure 21-5. *PowerBomber level 3*

You can see how the background buffer is drawn to the main buffer, then the game objects are drawn into the main buffer, and finally the main buffer is blasted out to the PowerShell console. PowerShell certainly wasn't built for this, but we made it work in the name of education and just because we can. 😊

Game Objects

Each game object is stored in its own text-based configuration file using the same method used for building out the levels. Each object configuration file contains the name, speed, height, width, and number of frames used for animation. Then the file contains the ASCII art used to draw the object and then finally a pair of tags: MOVESCRIPTSTART: AND MOVESCRIPTEND:. You can place PowerShell code between

203

these tags, and it will get executed between each frame in the game. The move scripts do exactly that, and you can use the code to move your objects around the game level and even throw in some AI techniques to make things more interesting for the player. Finally, game objects can include sound script tags to define what noises the objects make then they move or get blown up!

Standard Wall Block

Lets' first take a look at a standard wall block. We use the name to identify the object type in the game engine, since each object type may behave differently in the game. Wall blocks, for example, won't let a player walk through them or blow them up:

```
NAME:BLOCK
SPEED:0
HEIGHT:3
WIDTH:5
FRAMES:1
#####
#####
#####
MOVESCRIPTSTART:
MOVESCRIPTEND:
```

Explodable Wall Block

Explodable wall blocks will let the player blow them up to make them disappear:

```
NAME:BLOCK2
SPEED:0
HEIGHT:3
WIDTH:5
FRAMES:1
\/\/\
\/\/\
\/\/\
MOVESCRIPTSTART:
MOVESCRIPTEND:
```

Bombs

Bombs get placed by the player during gameplay when they press the space bar key, and since they are bombs, they need to do something when they explode. We could create an animation using multiple frames, but since the blast of the bomb can be stopped by walls, we need to make it more dynamic and control it using some extra code.

Let's take a closer look at how the explosion works, but review the following full code listing to see the full script.

When a bomb explodes, it creates a new object based on the GameObject class and loads a configuration file for it, which in this case is an explode object. This object is inserted into the game level, and the game engine simply runs the object's code during each frame of the game. What the explode object does is wait 400 milliseconds and then set its dead variable to $true. This tells the game engine to remove it from the game. So if we place an explode object around the bomb's location, we can generate the effect of the bomb exploding, and the game engine will handle the rest because it knows that if an explode object hits the player object, then the player gets killed in the game:

```
$Explode = New-Object GameObject
$Explode.LoadObject("Explode.txt")

#Place the bomb to the left of the player.
$Explode.xPosition = $this.xPosition - 10
$Explode.yPosition = $this.yPosition

#add the object to the levels object array
$global:levels[$global:currentLevel].objects += $Explode
```

Take some time to review the bomb object configuration file and study the move script file to work out exactly what it does during each frame of the game:

```
NAME:BOMB
SPEED:0
HEIGHT:3
WIDTH:5
FRAMES:1
/---\
| + |
\---/
```

```
MOVESCRIPTSTART:

if($this.timer.Elapsed.Seconds -ge 2)
{
    if($this.currentAnimationFrame -eq 0)
    {
        $this.PlaySound("EXPLODE")

        if($this.xPosition - 5 -ge 1)
            {
                $Explode = New-Object GameObject
                $Explode.LoadObject("Explode.txt")
                $Explode.xPosition = $this.xPosition - 5
                $Explode.yPosition = $this.yPosition
                    $Explode.OriginID  = $this.OriginID #pass the spawing
                    character down to the explosion objects
                    $Explode.SetupJob($global:levels[$global:currentLevel])
                $global:levels[$global:currentLevel].objects += $Explode
        }

        if($this.xPosition + 10 -le $global:displayWidth)
            {
                $Explode = New-Object GameObject
                $Explode.LoadObject("Explode.txt")
                $Explode.xPosition = $this.xPosition + 5
                $Explode.yPosition = $this.yPosition
                    $Explode.OriginID  = $this.OriginID #pass the spawing
                    character down to the explosion objects
                    $Explode.SetupJob($global:levels[$global:currentLevel])
                $global:levels[$global:currentLevel].objects += $Explode
            }

        if($this.yPosition - 3 -ge 4)
            {
                $Explode = New-Object GameObject
                $Explode.LoadObject("Explode.txt")
                $Explode.xPosition = $this.xPosition
```

```
                $Explode.yPosition = $this.yPosition - 3
                    $Explode.OriginID  = $this.OriginID #pass the spawing
                    character down to the explosion objects
                    $Explode.SetupJob($global:levels[$global:currentLevel])
                $global:levels[$global:currentLevel].objects += $Explode
        }

        if(($this.yPosition + 9) -lt $global:displayHeight)
            {
                $Explode = New-Object GameObject
                $Explode.LoadObject("Explode.txt")
                $Explode.xPosition = $this.xPosition
                $Explode.yPosition = $this.yPosition + 3
                    $Explode.OriginID  = $this.OriginID #pass the spawing
                    character down to the explosion objects
                    $Explode.SetupJob($global:levels[$global:currentLevel])
                $global:levels[$global:currentLevel].objects += $Explode
            }

        $this.currentAnimationFrame++
    }
}

if($this.timer.Elapsed.Seconds -ge 2 -and $this.timer.Elapsed.Milliseconds
-ge 600)
{
    if($this.currentAnimationFrame -eq 2)
    {
        if($this.xPosition - 5 -ge 1)
            {
            if($this.DoesCollide(($this.xPosition - 5),$this.yPosition,
            $this.objectHeight,$this.objectWidth) -eq $false)
            {
                $Explode = New-Object GameObject
                $Explode.LoadObject("Explode.txt")
                $Explode.xPosition = $this.xPosition - 10
                $Explode.yPosition = $this.yPosition
```

```
            $Explode.OriginID  = $this.OriginID #pass the spawing
            character down to the explosion objects
            $Explode.SetupJob($global:levels[$global:currentLevel])
        $global:levels[$global:currentLevel].objects += $Explode
    }
  }

if($this.xPosition + 10 -le $global:displayWidth)
    {
    if($this.DoesCollide(($this.xPosition + 5),$this.yPosition,
    $this.objectHeight,$this.objectWidth) -eq $false)
    {
        $Explode = New-Object GameObject
        $Explode.LoadObject("Explode.txt")
        $Explode.xPosition = $this.xPosition + 10
        $Explode.yPosition = $this.yPosition
            $Explode.OriginID  = $this.OriginID #pass the spawing
            character down to the explosion objects
            $Explode.SetupJob($global:levels[$global:currentLevel])
        $global:levels[$global:currentLevel].objects += $Explode
    }
  }

if($this.yPosition - 3 -ge 4)
    {
    if($this.DoesCollide($this.xPosition,($this.yPosition - 3),
    $this.objectHeight,$this.objectWidth) -eq $false)
    {
        $Explode = New-Object GameObject
        $Explode.LoadObject("Explode.txt")
        $Explode.xPosition = $this.xPosition
        $Explode.yPosition = $this.yPosition - 6
            $Explode.OriginID  = $this.OriginID #pass the spawing
            character down to the explosion objects
```

```
                    $Explode.SetupJob($global:levels[$global:currentLevel])
                    $global:levels[$global:currentLevel].objects += $Explode
            }
        }

        if(($this.yPosition + 10) -lt $global:displayHeight)
        {
        if($this.DoesCollide($this.xPosition,($this.yPosition + 3),
        $this.objectHeight,$this.objectWidth) -eq $false)
        {
            #$Explode.xPosition = $this.xPosition
            #$Explode.yPosition = $this.yPosition + 3

            $Explode = New-Object GameObject
            $Explode.LoadObject("Explode.txt")
            $Explode.xPosition = $this.xPosition
            $Explode.yPosition = $this.yPosition + 6
                $Explode.OriginID  = $this.OriginID #pass the spawing
                character down to the explosion objects
                $Explode.SetupJob($global:levels[$global:currentLevel])
            $global:levels[$global:currentLevel].objects += $Explode
        }
        }

        $this.currentAnimationFrame++
    }
}

if($this.timer.Elapsed.seconds -ge 2)
{
    $this.hidden = $true
}

if($this.timer.Elapsed.Seconds -ge 4)
{
    $this.dead = $true
}
```

```
MOVESCRIPTEND:

SOUNDSCRIPTSTART:
NAME:EXPLODE
[console]::beep(60,100)
[console]::beep(70,100)
[console]::beep(80,100)
[console]::beep(100,100)
[console]::beep(150,100)
[console]::beep(90,100)
[console]::beep(60,100)
[console]::beep(70,100)
SOUNDSCRIPTEND:
```

Code

Here is the full code listing for the main code for PowerBomber. Take some time to study it because reading other people's code and working out how it works is an important skill. During your time working with PowerShell, you will copy example scripts from the Internet and modify them for your own use, so taking time to study them carefully is vital.

```
using module '.\Modules\PathFinder.psm1'
using module '.\Modules\Level.psm1'
using module '.\Modules\GameObject.psm1'
using module '.\Modules\Sound.psm1'

#Variables#########################
$global:gameLoopRunning = $True
$global:exitGame = $false
$global:displayWidth = 107
$global:displayHeight = 52
$global:playerScore = 0
$global:highScore = 0
$global:currentLevel = -1
$global:gameLevelCount = 0
```

```
#Performance Metrics
$global:fps = 0
$global:frames = 0
$global:fpsTimer = New-Object -TypeName System.Diagnostics.Stopwatch
$global:totalFrames = 0 #used to trigger events that dont fire every frame

$global:titleScreen = ""
$global:gameOverScreen = ""
$global:endGameScreen = ""
$global:gameCompeteScreen = ""

[System.Collections.ArrayList]$global:screenBuffer = New-Object System.
Collections.ArrayList
[System.Collections.ArrayList]$global:backgroundBuffer = New-Object System.
Collections.ArrayList
[System.Collections.ArrayList]$global:levels = New-Object System.
Collections.ArrayList

[PathFinder]$global:pathFinder

#####################################

#Functions###########################################################
function Load-Level([string]$file) {
    [Array]$buffer = @()

    #read lines and loop through each line
    Get-Content $file | ForEach-Object {
        $buffer += $_
    }

    return $buffer
}

function Setup-Display([int]$width, [int] $height) {
    $psHost = get-host
    $window = $psHost.ui.rawui
    $newSize = $window.windowsize
    $newSize.height = $height
```

```powershell
    $newSize.width = $width
    $window.windowsize = $newSize
}

function Read-Character() {

    if ([console]::KeyAvailable) {
        return $Host.UI.RawUI.ReadKey("NoEcho,IncludeKeyDown").Character
    }

    return $null
}

function Clear-ScreenBuffer() {
    for ($i = 0; $i -lt 110; $i++) {
        $null = $global:screenBuffer.Add(@(""))
    }
}
function Move-Cursor([int]$x, [int] $y) {
    $host.UI.RawUI.CursorPosition = New-Object System.Management.
    Automation.Host.Coordinates $x , $y
}
function Spawn-Bomb([Guid]$oID, [int]$x, [int] $y) {
    $bomb = New-Object GameObject
    $bomb.LoadObject("Bomb.txt")
    $bomb.xPosition = $x
    $bomb.yPosition = $y
    $bomb.OriginID = $oID
    $bomb.SetupJob($global:levels[$global:currentLevel])
    $global:levels[$global:currentLevel].objects += $bomb
}

function Read-PlayerInput() {
    #See what keys the player is pressing
    $char = Read-Character
```

```
$global:levels[$global:currentLevel].objects[0].xPositionOld =
$global:levels[$global:currentLevel].objects[0].xPosition;
$global:levels[$global:currentLevel].objects[0].yPositionOld =
$global:levels[$global:currentLevel].objects[0].yPosition;

if ($char -eq 'q') {
    $global:exitGame = $True
    $global:gameLoopRunning = $False
}
elseif ($char -eq 'a') {
    $global:levels[$global:currentLevel].objects[0].PlaySound("MOVE")
    $global:levels[$global:currentLevel].objects[0].xPosition -= 5
}
elseif ($char -eq 'd') {
    $global:levels[$global:currentLevel].objects[0].PlaySound("MOVE")
    $global:levels[$global:currentLevel].objects[0].xPosition += 5
}
elseif ($char -eq 'w') {
    $global:levels[$global:currentLevel].objects[0].PlaySound("MOVE")
    $global:levels[$global:currentLevel].objects[0].yPosition -= 3
}
elseif ($char -eq 's') {
    $global:levels[$global:currentLevel].objects[0].PlaySound("MOVE")
    $global:levels[$global:currentLevel].objects[0].yPosition += 3
}
elseif ($char -eq ' ') {
    Spawn-Bomb $global:levels[$global:currentLevel].objects[0].ID
    ($global:levels[$global:currentLevel].objects[0].xPosition)
    ($global:levels[$global:currentLevel].objects[0].yPosition)
}
elseif ($char -eq 't') {
}
```

```
    #Keep player inside the display
    if ($global:levels[$global:currentLevel].objects[0].xPosition -le 0) {
        $global:levels[$global:currentLevel].objects[0].xPosition = 1
    }
    elseif ($global:levels[$global:currentLevel].objects[0].xPosition -ge
    $global:displayWidth - $global:levels[$global:currentLevel].objects[0].
    objectWidth) {
        $global:levels[$global:currentLevel].objects[0].xPosition =
        $global:displayWidth - $global:levels[$global:currentLevel].
        objects[0].objectWidth - 1
    }

    if ($global:levels[$global:currentLevel].objects[0].yPosition -le 5) {
        $global:levels[$global:currentLevel].objects[0].yPosition = 5
    }
    elseif ($global:levels[$global:currentLevel].objects[0].yPosition
    -ge ($global:displayHeight - $global:levels[$global:currentLevel].
    objects[0].objectHeight) - 2) {
        $global:levels[$global:currentLevel].objects[0].yPosition =
        ($global:displayHeight - $global:levels[$global:currentLevel].
        objects[0].objectHeight - 2)
    }
}
function Remove-DeadObjects() {
    $totalDead = 0
    for ($i = 0; $i -lt $global:levels[$global:currentLevel].objects.Count;
    $i++) {
        if ($global:levels[$global:currentLevel].objects[$i].IsDead()) {
            $totalDead++
        }
    }

    if ($totalDead -eq 0) {
        return
    }
```

```
    for ($i = 0; $i -lt $global:levels[$global:currentLevel].objects.Count;
    $i++) {
        if ($global:levels[$global:currentLevel].objects[$i].IsDead()) {
            $global:levels[$global:currentLevel].objects.RemoveAt($i)
        }
    }

    Remove-DeadObjects
}

function Collide($objectA, $objectB) {
    if ($objectA.IsDead() -or $objectB.IsDead()) {
        return $false
    }

    [bool]$collide = $false

    #speed increase#########
    if (($objectA.xPosition + $objectA.objectWidth) -lt $objectB.xPosition) {
        return $collide
    }

    if ($objectA.xPosition -gt ($objectB.xPosition + $objectB.objectWidth)) {
        return $collide
    }

    if (($objectA.yPosition + $objectA.objectHeight) -lt $objectB.
    yPosition) {
        return $collide
    }

    if ($objectA.yPosition -gt ($objectB.yPosition + $objectB.object.
    Height)) {
        return $collide
    }
    #######################
```

```
    if ($objectA.xPosition -lt ($objectB.xPosition + $objectB.objectWidth)
    -and ($objectA.xPosition + $objectA.objectWidth) -gt $objectB.
    xPosition -and $objectA.yPosition -lt ($objectB.yPosition + $objectB.
    objectHeight) -and ($objectA.objectHeight + $objectA.yPosition) -gt
    $objectB.yPosition) {
        $collide = $true
    }

    return $false #$collide
}

function Check-ForCollisions() {
    $cLevel = $global:levels[$global:currentLevel]

    #check for object collisions (treat all collisions as deaths)
    for ($i = 0; $i -lt $cLevel.objects.Count; $i++) {
        $iObject = $cLevel.objects[$i]

        for ($j = ($i + 1); $j -lt $cLevel.objects.Count; $j++) {
            $jObject = $cLevel.objects[$j]

            #write-host $iObject.name $jObject.name
            if (($iObject.name -eq "BOMB" -and $jObject.name -eq "ENEMY")
            -or ($iObject.name -eq "ENEMY" -and $jObject.name -eq "BOMB")) {
                #dont cause a collision when an enemy player drops a bomb
                on their current location
            }
            elseif (($iObject.name -eq "BOMB" -and $jObject.name -eq
            "PLAYER") -or ($iObject.name -eq "PLAYER" -and $jObject.name -eq
            "BOMB")) {
                #dont cause a collision when a player drops a bomb on their
                current location
            }
            elseif (($iObject.name -eq "EXPLODE" -and $jObject.name -eq
            "BLOCK") -or ($iObject.name -eq "BLOCK" -and $jObject.name -eq
            "EXPLODE")) {
                #dont cause a collision when an explosion hits a block
                because they cant be destroyed
            }
```

```
elseif (($iObject.name -eq "BLOCK" -and $jObject.name -eq
"BLOCK2") -or ($iObject.name -eq "BLOCK2" -and $jObject.name
-eq "BLOCK")) {
    #dont cause a collision when blocks overlap
}
elseif (($iObject.name -eq "EXPLODE" -and $jObject.name -eq
"PORTAL") -or ($iObject.name -eq "PORTAL" -and $jObject.name
-eq "EXPLODE")) {
    #dont cause a collision when blocks overlap
}
else {
    if ($iObject.IsDead() -or $jObject.IsDead()) {

    }
    elseif ($iObject.xPosition -lt ($jObject.xPosition +
    $jObject.objectWidth) -and ($iObject.xPosition + $iObject.
    objectWidth) -gt $jObject.xPosition -and $iObject.yPosition
    -lt ($jObject.yPosition + $jObject.objectHeight) -and
    ($iObject.objectHeight + $iObject.yPosition) -gt $jObject.
    yPosition) { #)#Collide $iObject $jObject)
        if ($iObject.name -eq "PLAYER" -and $jObject.name -eq
        "BLOCK") {
            #Player cant move into a block position so set
            player back to previous position
            $cLevel.objects[0].xPosition = $cLevel.objects[0].
            xPositionOld;
            $cLevel.objects[0].yPosition = $cLevel.objects[0].
            yPositionOld;
        }
        elseif ($iObject.name -eq "PLAYER" -and $jObject.name
        -eq "BLOCK2") {
            #Player cant move into a block position so set
            player back to previous position
            $cLevel.objects[0].xPosition = $cLevel.objects[0].
            xPositionOld;
```

```
            $cLevel.objects[0].yPosition = $cLevel.objects[0].
            yPositionOld;
    }
    elseif ($iObject.name -eq "EXPLODE" -and $jObject.name
    -eq "BLOCK") {
        #if an explosion hits a block do nothing
    }
    elseif ($iObject.name -eq "EXPLODE" -and $jObject.name
    -eq "BLOCK2") {
        if ($global:levels[$global:currentLevel].
        objects[0].ID -eq $iObject.OriginID) {
            $global:playerScore += 1
        }

        #write-host "player score" -ForegroundColor Red
        #pause

        $cLevel.objects[$i].DoDeath()
        $cLevel.objects[$j].DoDeath()
    }
    elseif ($iObject.name -eq "BLOCK2" -and $jObject.name
    -eq "EXPLODE") {
        if ($global:levels[$global:currentLevel].
        objects[0].ID -eq $jObject.OriginID) {
            $global:playerScore += 1
        }

        $cLevel.objects[$i].DoDeath()
        $cLevel.objects[$j].DoDeath()
    }
    elseif ($iObject.name -eq "PLAYER" -and $jObject.name
    -eq "PORTAL") {
        #Player cant move into a block position so set
        player back to previous position
        $jObject.DoDeath()
    }
```

```
                elseif ($iObject.name -eq "PORTAL" -and $jObject.name
                -eq "PLAYER") {
                    #Player cant move into a block position so set
                    player back to previous position
                    $iObject.DoDeath()
                }
                else {
                    $cLevel.objects[$i].DoDeath()
                    $cLevel.objects[$j].DoDeath()
                }
            }
        }
    }
}

function Run-GameLogic() {
    Read-PlayerInput

    #run game objects run logic
    for ($i = 1; $i -lt $global:levels[$global:currentLevel].objects.Count;
    $i++) {
        $global:levels[$global:currentLevel].objects[$i].RunLogic()
    }

    Check-ForCollisions
}

function Player-Dead() {
    #Display game over screen and wait for player to confirm restart
    $global:backgroundBuffer = Load-Level $global:gameOverScreen
    Clear-ScreenBuffer
    Move-Cursor 0 0
    Draw-BackgroundtoScreenBuffer
    Draw-Buffer
```

```
    Start-Sleep -s 2
    $Host.UI.RawUI.FlushInputBuffer()

    $global:gameLoopRunning = $false

    if ($global:playerScore -gt $global:highScore) {
        $global:highScore = $global:playerScore
    }

    $global:playerScore = 0

    #Wait for user to press any key
    $continue = $host.UI.RawUI.ReadKey("NoEcho,IncludeKeyDown")
}

function Detect-LevelWinOld() {
    $win = $true

    if ($global:levels[$global:currentLevel].objects[0].IsDead()) {
        $win = $false
    }

    for ($i = 0; $i -lt $global:levels[$global:currentLevel].objects.Count;
    $i++) {
        if ($global:levels[$global:currentLevel].objects[$i].name -eq
        "ENEMY") { # -and $global:levels[$global:currentLevel].objects[$i].
        isDead() -eq $true)
            $win = $false
        }
    }

    return $win
}

function Detect-LevelWin() {
    $win = $true

    if ($global:levels[$global:currentLevel].objects[0].IsDead()) {
        $win = $false
    }
```

```
    for ($i = 0; $i -lt $global:levels[$global:currentLevel].objects.Count;
    $i++) {
        if ($global:levels[$global:currentLevel].objects[$i].name -eq
        "PORTAL") {
            $win = $false
        }
    }

    return $win
}
function Load-NextLevel() {
    Clear-Host

    $global:currentLevel++

    if ($global:currentLevel -lt $global:gameLevelCount) {
        #Start-Sleep -s 1
        Move-Cursor 47 27
        Write-Host "Level: " ($global:currentLevel + 1)
        $global:backgroundBuffer = Load-Level $global:levels[$global:
        ].background

        #setup path finder for level
        $global:pathFinder = new-object PathFinder($host, $global:levels
        [$global:currentLevel], $global:displayWidth,
        ($global:displayHeight - 1), 5, 3)

        Start-Sleep -s 3
    }
}

function Load-GameConfig($gameConfig) {
    #Read file content into lines
    $lines = Get-Content $gameConfig
    $global:titleScreen = $lines[0].Split(':')[1]
    $global:gameOverScreen = $lines[1].Split(':')[1]
    $global:endGameScreen = $lines[2].Split(':')[1]
    $global:gameCompleteScreen = $lines[3].Split(':')[1]
```

```
$global:levels = New-Object System.Collections.ArrayList
$global:gameLevelCount = 0

for ($i = 0; $i -lt $lines.Length; $i++) {
    if ($lines[$i] -eq "STARTLEVEL:") {
        $global:levels += New-Object Level
        $levelObjectCount = 0
        $i++
        while ($lines[$i] -ne "ENDLEVEL:") {
            if ($lines[$i].StartsWith("NAME:",
            "CurrentCultureIgnoreCase")) {
                $global:levels[$global:gameLevelCount].name =
                $lines[$i].Split(':')[1]
            }
            elseif ($lines[$i].StartsWith("BACKGROUND:",
            "CurrentCultureIgnoreCase")) {
                $global:levels[$global:gameLevelCount].background =
                $lines[$i].Split(':')[1]
            }
            elseif ($lines[$i].StartsWith("SPAWN:",
            "CurrentCultureIgnoreCase")) {
                $index = $global:levels[$global:gameLevelCount].
                objects.Add((New-Object GameObject))
                $global:levels[$global:gameLevelCount].
                objects[$levelObjectCount].LoadObject($lines[$i].
                Split(':')[1])
                $global:levels[$global:gameLevelCount].
                objects[$levelObjectCount].xPosition = $lines[$i].
                Split(':')[3]
                $global:levels[$global:gameLevelCount].
                objects[$levelObjectCount].yPosition = $lines[$i].
                Split(':')[4]
                $global:levels[$global:gameLevelCount].
                objects[$levelObjectCount].SetupJob($global:levels
                [$global:gameLevelCount])
```

```
                $levelObjectCount++
            }

            $i++
        }
        $global:gameLevelCount++
    }
  }
}

function Draw-BackgroundtoScreenBuffer() {
    For ($i = 0; $i -lt $global:screenBuffer.Count; $i++) {
        $global:screenBuffer[$i] = $global:backgroundBuffer[$i]
    }
}

function Draw-ObjectstoScreenBuffer() {
    Draw-BackgroundtoScreenBuffer

    #draw game objects
    #For($i = 0;$i -lt $global:levels[$global:currentLevel].objects.
    Count;$i++)
    #{
    #    $global:levels[$global:currentLevel].objects[$i].DrawObject(
    $global:screenBuffer)
    #}

    foreach ($obj in $global:levels[$global:currentLevel].objects) {
        $obj.DrawObject($global:screenBuffer)
    }

    #update score
    Write-ScreenBuffer 3 1 "FPS: $global:fps"
    Write-ScreenBuffer 3 2 "High Score: $global:highScore"
    Write-ScreenBuffer 3 3 "Player Score: $global:playerScore"
}
```

```
function Write-ScreenBuffer([int]$x, [int]$y, [string]$text) {
    $global:screenBuffer[$y] = $global:screenBuffer[$y].Remove($x, $text.
    Length).Insert($x, $text)
}

function Draw-Buffer() {
    $global:screenBuffer
}

function Detect-GameWin() {
    if ($global:currentLevel -eq $global:gameLevelCount) {
        $global:gameLoopRunning = $false

        #Display title screen and wait for player to confirm start
        $global:backgroundBuffer = Load-Level $global:gameCompleteScreen

        Clear-ScreenBuffer
        Move-Cursor 0 0
        DrawBackgroundtoScreenBuffer
        DrawBuffer

        Start-Sleep -s 3

        $global:gameLoopRunning = $false

        if ($global:playerScore -gt $global:highScore) {
            $global:highScore = $global:playerScore
        }

        $global:playerScore = 0

        #Wait for user to press any key
        $Host.UI.RawUI.FlushInputBuffer()
        $continue = $host.UI.RawUI.ReadKey("NoEcho,IncludeKeyDown")
    }
}
###########################################################################
```

```
#Start Running Program Commands

#Clear screen
Clear-Host

#Set powershell console windowto required size
Setup-Display $global:displayWidth $global:displayHeight

while (!$global:exitGame) {
    #Clear screen and initialise global variables
    Clear-Host
    $global:currentLevel = -1
    $global:gameLoopRunning = $True
    $global:backgroundBuffer = @()
    $global:screenBuffer = @()
    Load-GameConfig("GameConfig.txt")

    #Display title screen and wait for player to confirm start
    $global:backgroundBuffer = Load-Level "TitleScreen.txt"
    Clear-ScreenBuffer
    Move-Cursor 0 0
    Draw-BackgroundtoScreenBuffer
    Draw-Buffer

    #Wait for user to press any key
    $Host.UI.RawUI.FlushInputBuffer()
    $continue = $host.UI.RawUI.ReadKey("NoEcho,IncludeKeyDown")

    Load-NextLevel

    $global:fpsTimer.Start()
    while ($global:gameLoopRunning) {
        Move-Cursor 0 0
        Draw-ObjectstoScreenBuffer
        Draw-Buffer

        Run-GameLogic
```

```powershell
    #See if player got killed and restart game
    if ($global:levels[$global:currentLevel].objects[0].IsDead()) {
        Player-Dead
    }
    else {

        Remove-DeadObjects

        #Check to see if player has won the level
        if (Detect-LevelWin -eq $true) {
            #level up
            Load-NextLevel
            Detect-GameWin
        }

        $global:frames++
        if ($global:fpsTimer.Elapsed.Seconds -ge 1) {
            $global:fps = $global:frames
            $global:frames = 0
            $global:fpsTimer.Restart()
        }

        $global:totalFrames++
    }
  }
}

#Display close screen
$global:backgroundBuffer = Load-Level "QuitScreen.txt"
Clear-ScreenBuffer
Move-Cursor 0 0
Draw-BackgroundtoScreenBuffer
Draw-Buffer

Start-Sleep -s 2

#Clear screen
Clear-Host
```

Conclusion

I don't think PowerShell was meant to do that, but hey, we made it work, learned some new stuff, and became even more confident in using PowerShell.

I would love to see some of your own games, so please send them over to me: ian@slashadmin.co.uk.

I'll post all appropriate submissions to my blog and share with everyone.

I hope this book has helped you on your journey to becoming a PowerShell master and did it in a different and fun way.

I look forward to seeing what you come up with in the future and good luck!

Index

© Ian Waters 2021
I. Waters, *PowerShell for Beginners*, https://doi.org/10.1007/978-1-4842-7064-6

U

User input
  key presses, 97–99
  line of text, 99, 100
  return value, 98
  script code, 98

V, W, X, Y, Z

Variables, 33
  access code, 38
  definition, 36, 37
  global variables, 39, 40
  meaning, 35
  scope, 39
  types, 35, 36
  update option, 37
Visual Studio code
  comment sections
    code, 31

help option, 31, 32
  multi lines, 32
  single-line comment, 32
extensions, 21, 22
installation, 16–18
meaning, 16
project folder, 18, 19
script file, 20
scripts
  break points, 26
  configuration file, 25
  confirmation, 23–25
  console window, 23
  control panel, 28
  debugging tools, 24–29
  launch.json file, 26
  running option, 23, 24
  saving option, 22
  terminal window, 30, 31
  test part selection, 29, 30

Printed in the United States
by Baker & Taylor Publisher Services